down the Copland Road

RONNIE ESPLIN

Argyll
publishing

First published 2000
Argyll Publishing
Glendaruel
Argyll PA22 3AE
Scotland

The author has asserted his
moral rights.

**British Library
Cataloguing-in-
Publication Data.
A catalogue record for
this book is available
from the British
Library.**

ISBN 1 902831 14 4

Cover Photos
Courtesy Scottish Daily
Record & Sunday Mail Ltd

Origination
Cordfall Ltd, Glasgow

Printing
Omnia Books Limited,
Glasgow

To my wife Anne
and my children,
Kirsty, Alexander and Mhairi

Acknowledgements

THANKS go the academic heavyweights
Graham Walker and Bill Murray whose
sterling work in similar and related fields
underpinned much of this book.

I am grateful to Colin Glass for acting as
a sounding board and whose knowledge of
all things Rangers was invaluable.

Thanks also to Jim Traynor, Bill Leckie,
Iain King, Simon Stone, Ian McColl,
Raymond Boyle and Tony Higgins who all
took time out of their busy schedules to
contribute.

Thanks also to editor and publisher
Derek Rodger for offering support and
advice.

Last and of course not least, thanks to
all the fans who took time to answer the
questions.

Ronnie Esplin

Contents

Respondents

Grant Aitchison	Bellshill Chosen Few	Ian McColl	Black Bull RSC
John Allardyce	Cambuslang	Davie MacDonald	Irvine and District RSC
Ronnie Bayne	Gilmour French Mem.	Peter McDonald	Glasgow
Jim Black	Ayrshire	Robert McElroy	Glasgow
Julian Brent	Leeds	Allan McEwan	Toby Jug True Blues
Iain Breslin	Fife	Ian McHutchison	Hawick
Dougie Brown	Glasgow	Charlie McIntyre	Campbeltown
Willie Buchan	Bellshill Chosen Few	Peter McFarlane	Lanarkshire
Neil Cameron	Lockerbie RSC	Wull McLay	Coalburn
Ian Campbell	Galashiels RSC	Derek McLeod	Perth
John Carroll	Paisley	Stephen McLeod	Lewis
Dugald Clark	New Zealand	Alan McNamara	Kinning Park Loyal
David Collins	Port Glasgow	Andrew Nesbitt	Manchester RSC
Stuart Crichton	Toronto	Dave Nicol	Glasgow
Stuart Daniels	Kinning Park Loyal	Tanya Orr	Gatehouse of Fleet
Alison Dempster	Ayr	Tony Orr	London
Graham Donaldson	Paisley	Alan Park	Clarkston RSC
Brian Donaghy	Castle Street RSC	Kirsty Paterson	Kinross
Allan Elder	Nairn	Dougie Patterson	Dumbarton
Adam Elder	Springhall	Gary Paul	Inverness
Peter Ewart	Northern Ireland	Richard Pollock	Toby Jug True Blues
Drew Failes	Dennistoun	Tom Plunkett	NARSA (Florida)
John Frame	Honest Toun RSC	Bob Prescott	Alexandria
Graham Gardner	Kilmarnock	Chris Rae	Renfrew
Frank Geddes	Invergordon RSC	Ally Redford	Stoke-on-Trent RSC
Colin Glass	Bearsden	Jimmy Reid	Beith Saracen RSC
Scott Graham	Linwood	Jim Reid	Stewarton
Gordon Graham	Glasgow	Alan Russell	Glasgow
Derek Inglis	Fernhill Loyal RSC	Angelique Shield	Glasgow
Gordon Inglis	Springhall	Alan Smith	Glasgow
Rhys Jones	Northern Ireland	Rab Smith	Melbourne RSC
Fiona Kell	Carlisle	Gordon Stewart	Campsie Loyal RSC
Andrew Kerr	Northern Ireland	Dave Taylor	Carluke
Craig Knox	Campsie Loyal RSC	Willie Torrie	Hawick RSC
Garry Lynch	Cambuslang	Alan Urquhart	Mayfield & N'grange
Gordon Masterton	Kingston-uponThames	Alistair Walker	Zurich
John Macmillan	Rangers Supp. Assoc	Des Ward	Orkney
Stevie Mochrie	Castlecary	Mike Watt	Granite City RSC
Richard Morrier	Glasgow	Eddie Wood	Blairbeth
Alan Morton	Mayfield & N'grange	Brian Whitelaw	NARSA (Ontario)
Derek McAvoy	London	Ally Williamson	Glasgow
Harry McCallum	Rozental Loyal		

1

Introduction

WHO ARE the supporters of Scotland's largest and most successful club? What are their opinions and where do they stand at this time of great changes in football and in the wider social and political sphere? Having developed an interest in the whole history of football supporters' associations, it seemed a natural extension to think about one of Scotland's most visible groups of supporters. But where to start?

The writer Alan Spence characterised, if not caricatured, Rangers fans, most notably in his 1977 novel *Its Colours They Are Fine*.[1] Set in the 1950s and early 60s, the fictional characters represented a Protestant working class lifestyle within a Scottish society which had changed little from the turn of the twentieth century. Located against a Glasgow backdrop of tenements, shipyards, alcohol and poverty, it was Ibrox which provided the weekend release for the protagonists.

Protestantism then still had influence in many areas of Scottish society and most Rangers fans had some sort of tangible bond with their local Church. And there were tensions between Protestants and Catholics. Postwar Celtic fans could not have been accused of being paranoid – there *was* anti-Catholic discrimination in many areas of Scottish society, especially in sectors of industry.

Politically, it was a two horse race in Scotland. Labour and the Conservatives fought for the spoils in a country still strongly supportive of the Union. The Home Rule brigade were at their lowest ebb and a dormant form of Scottish nationalism, which sat as comfortably at Ibrox as anywhere, existed without threatening the British political system.

Although the print media had their interest in football, the unrestrained age of live radio and television had yet to arrive. Football was very much a spectator sport and indeed it was in the 1950s that many clubs registered their record attendances.[2]

The Rangers Supporters Association had emerged and was developing after a period of quiet as far as organised football groups were concerned.[3] It was the heyday of fans travelling on supporters buses and there was more of a local hue to the Rangers support than is evident in more recent years.[4]

On the pitch, the Ibrox club were successful but not to the recent extent of monopolising the Scottish game. There was a more parochial attitude to football in Scotland. European club football was emerging, but had yet to rival the domestic game. Glamour occasions came in the annual Scotland versus England game where there was traditionally a strong Rangers presence both on the park and on the terracing. Thus, it was in this context that Rangers fans were last chronicled.

But Scottish society and Scottish football have undergone massive changes in the intervening decades and this book's remit is to explore how Rangers fans have affected and been affected by all these developments. It has been difficult to separate these issues into individual stand-alone chapters as overlaps occur in many cases. Religion, unsurprisingly, appears in several chapters as does Mr Graeme Souness, surely one of the most significant figures in Ibrox history. It is hoped that any overlap or repetition has been kept to a minimum.

Chapter 2 examines the link between Protestantism and the identity of Rangers fans in an increasingly secular Scotland. Formal links between the Protestant Churches and Rangers FC are almost non-existent and Chairman David Murray has attempted to eradicate the negativity that the religious identity of the club inspires. What exactly is the Ibrox fans' present relationship with religion? The fans reveal their thoughts in addition to explaining the complexities behind the controversial songs still being sung by many Rangers supporters.

Chapter 3 explores the long-held beliefs that most Rangers fans are Conservative voters and that Ibrox is a safe haven for extreme right wing groups. What the fans have to say explodes these views as myths. Traditionally seen as supporters of the Union and the Royal Family, how do Rangers supporters react to the increasing drive for independence and the threat to the future of the monarchy?

Chapter 4 brings out the relationship between Rangers fans and the Scotland international set-up and the distrust that exists between Rangers fans the the Scottish Football Association. The bizarre identity battle – *Rule Britannia/Flower of Scotland* – that gets fought out in the stands of grounds all over the country is explained.

Chapter 5 brings up the commercial pressures that bear in on football and its effect on the club. The making of money has become, in the eyes of many fans, the most important part of their club. The commercial boom and its effect on on-field performance at the beginning of the 1990s was welcomed by most at Ibrox. But a decade on, what do the Rangers fans now feel about the issue of money in football?

Chapter 6 continues the discussion of the commercial pressures and what the future holds for the game in Scotland and Rangers' role within it. The future for the Ibrox club may be in a wider arena as proposals for various types of European leagues are now on the agenda.

Chapter 7 looks at Rangers fans perception of a hostile media and examines the credibility of those claims.

In Chapter 8, the bonds of the fans to Rangers Football Club are expressed. It is what following football is all about, after all. Supporters reflect on what makes them Rangers fans.

But who are the modern day Rangers fans? Well, there are supporters who are famous like Andy Cameron and Jonathan Watson but there are also 'famous' Rangers supporters like Stuart Daniels and Garry Lynch. Stuart has been abroad over seventy times to watch Rangers, including fifteen trips to Germany, six to Spain, five to Italy and three to Portugal as well as excursions behind the former Iron Curtain. Founder member of the Kinning Park Loyal RSC in 1976, Stuart said, 'It was written in the stars that I was going to be a Rangers fan. I was born a mile from the stadium, within the sound of the Ibrox roar, on the 20th of August 1947. Old Ibrox Park was opened on the 20th August 1887. So there was never any doubt.'[5]

Garry Lynch's devotion to Rangers is legendary amongst the supporters. Garry has missed only a handful of games since 1978. In one season in the mid-nineties he watched Rangers in the Premier League, Reserve League, Reserve League West and Youth League, an incredible 143 times. Garry said, 'Following your team, that's what it's all about. I admire guys who support Partick or Alloa or Stenhousemuir who, if they get promotion or a couple of seasons in the Premier league, are delighted. Some of the people you meet when you're abroad with Rangers and some of the supporters who come to Ibrox are brilliant.'[6]

Daniels and Lynch are not typical fans of course and the vast majority of supporters exhibit differing levels of enthusiasm and commitment to the Ibrox cause. Indeed, defining a Rangers fan may be more difficult than one might imagine, especially if you accept Ibrox chairman David Murray's claim that there are around a million Rangers fans, with only ten to fifteen percent of those having actually set foot inside Ibrox.[7]

At present, many fans are members of diverse organisations such as the Rangers Supporters Association (RSA), overseas supporters associations such as the North American Rangers Supporters Association (NARSA)[8] and in keeping with the new technological age, the 'Internet Loyal'.[9] And of course many supporters clubs operate outwith these organisations and there are many fans who belong to no supporters clubs or organisations.[10]

Given that there are Rangers fans all over the world it would take a huge football census to ascertain all their views on the subjects raised in this book. Thus, although care was taken to get a cross-section of fans, it is not an exhaustive study and makes no claims as such. Fans who wanted to give their opinions were allowed to do so.

Respondents were sought in several ways: through adverts in the *Rangers News*, in the Rangers fanzine *Number One* and through leaflets distributed before matches at Ibrox. Rangers supporters clubs' officials were targeted and the rather unscientific, but nonetheless enjoyable, task of talking to fans in pubs and clubs was also undertaken. Contacting fans overseas was made much easier and cheaper by new technology and adverts on the official Rangers website www.rangers.co.uk and on the unofficial website Rangers@fromtheterrace.co.uk were well received. Through this, a network built up into a diverse group of supporters who were willing to be quoted on the issues addressed in the book.

Interviews were mostly unstructured and ranged from short phone calls to long lunches and some answers were sent via e-mail. Some fans answered on a few topics and some were happy to answer questions on all the topics. Not every answer received appears in the book. For brevity, as well as attempting to make the book as enjoyable and interesting a read as possible, I have tried to provide a suitably weighted balance of opinions.

But while it is all well and good noting Rangers fans in terms of their different types and levels of support, it is individual supporters we turn to in order to determine thoughts on the issues involved in being a Rangers supporter. Alan Spence's works can arguably be taken as a representation of Rangers fans in postwar Scotland. This book, set in the new millennium, attempts a similar snapshot. Hopefully, the responses will be the first words on the important contemporary issues facing Rangers fans – not the last.

Ronnie Esplin
Glasgow, April 2000

2

Rangers Fans and Religion

ALTHOUGH the connection in many cases may be by default, Rangers FC and their fans are so inextricably linked with Protestantism, that it is almost impossible in Scotland to discuss one without referring to the other. But why did Rangers first assume the identity of the Protestant football club in Scotland? And why does this connection still linger in the minds of many supporters?

The 'success' of the Reformation in sixteenth century Scotland meant that by the end of the eighteenth century there were in fact few Catholics left in the country. In 1795 in Glasgow, where later religious tensions would be focused, their number was only 50.[1] Anti-Catholicism remained dormant in Scotland but there were few tensions between the two disparate religious groups. Protestants were kept busy with their own internal battles and indeed, since the time of John Knox, 'the major religious disputes in the country had been fought within the parameters of Protestantism'.[2]

However, the industrial revolution signalled the beginning of the revival of Catholicism in Scotland, 'and as the economy boomed, the consequent demand for labour was met in part by

Irish immigrants'.[3] Most of the new arrivals were Irish Catholics and the consequent resentment they encountered from the indigineous Scottish Protestants resulted in religious pressures, remnants of which remain in Scotland to this day.

The ghettoisation of the incoming Catholics impacted in all areas of Scottish society and sport, which became popular during the 'muscular Christianity' ethos of Victorian Britain, was no different. Such was the animosity of their Protestant hosts, it is perhaps understandable that Catholics, 'tended to remain within their own ethnic groups even when forming clubs for the playing of sport'.[4] The most public and durable examples of this exclusivity occurred in football.

Hibernian, founded in 1875, were the first and the most political Irish Catholic team in Scotland, closely identified with the issue of Home Rule (for Ireland) and part of its constitution was that, 'its players had to be practising Catholics'.[5] Celtic's inception thirteen years later, as well as including the charity aspect which dominates the Parkhead club's historical rhetoric, was based on a Catholic identity. Brother Walfred, founder of Celtic in 1888 was, 'worried about the dangers of young Catholics meeting Protestants after work and by the fear the Protestant soup kitchens might tempt them into apostasy'.[6] Thus, religious division was almost woven into the fabric of Scottish football in the early days. Other Catholic football teams were to emerge (then expire) in other areas in Scotland, notably Dundee, but the Edinburgh and Glasgow clubs became the two most important footballing vanguards of Catholicism in Scotland.

After their formation Celtic were immediately successful and had soon taken over Hibernian's crown of the top Catholic team in Scotland. Given the anti-Catholic feeling at the time it is no surprise that Celtic's success was not well received. Scottish society demanded a Protestant team to redress the balance and it was Rangers who emerged as suitable candidates.

Rangers Football Club was not formed as an extension of a religious community. Even the name, taken from an English rugby club, displayed a religious and political neutrality. They were primarily a football team and like other clubs who emerged in Glasgow like Clyde and Partick Thistle, 'they were Protestant only in the sense that a vast majority of clubs in Scotland at that time were made up of Protestants'.[7]

Queens Park may have taken up the Catholic Celtic challenge, if they had not stuck to their amateur ways which saw them left behind in the new developing professional football scene. (One of life's more surreal thoughts is Hampden Park packed out with 50,000 Spiders fans every other week.) Clyde and Partick Thistle could also perhaps have come to the fore as Scotland's Protestant representatives, but they simply weren't good enough at that time.

When Rangers beat Celtic four times and drew with them once, out of six games in 1893/94, a feat not yet seen, a 'worthy' Protestant team was born and 'supporters deserted the less successful clubs of Dunbartonshire, Lanarkshire and Renfrew and made the trek to Glasgow to encourage the team that seemed capable of stemming the emerald tide'.[8] A rivalry developed which was to eclipse the rest of Scottish football for the century since.

Although hard evidence is scarce, it is likely that Rangers Protestant image was strengthened when Harland and Wolfe, the Belfast shipping company, opened up in Govan in 1912 with a resultant influx of Ulster Protestants to the area. Rangers, having moved to the original Ibrox site in 1887, were therefore well-placed to attract the hordes of skilled workers who flocked to the increasingly popular game.[9] The 'local' nature of Rangers' Protestantism was supplemented by the wider religious tensions which increasingly permeated Scottish society to the extent that the interwar period was 'arguably Scotland's most intense period of sectarian animosity since the seventeenth century'.[10]

The anti-Irish element in Scottish society was intensified by the Irish quest for Home Rule which brought the Ulster Protestants in Scotland, especially Orange Order members, onto the streets to protest.[11] Political as well as religious divides deepened as Celtic and their fans supported Home Rule whereas their Ibrox rivals put their support behind the Union. The polarisation of the two communities was further exacerbated when the 1918 Education Act gave Catholics separate state-funded schools and thus, 'provoked predictable outrage from sections of Protestant opinion in Scotland'.[12] There were attempts to tap into the Protestant discontent and political parties were set up such as the Scottish Protestant League in 1920[13] and the Orange and Protestant Political Party in 1922.[14] However, it was anything but a marginalised discontent as the more established Unionist Party, 'gave overt political expression to the fears and prejudices of many Protestant Scots'.[15]

What was also important was that Protestant Church leaders, still influential in society, also played the anti-Catholic card. Between 1922 and 1938 the Presbyterian churches mounted a systematic campaign against Irish immigrants and Roman Catholics of Irish descent'.[16] The General Assembly of the Church of Scotland claimed that Catholics were 'undermining the purity of the Scots race'.[17] Thus, Scottish society in general was anti-Catholic and it was in this climate that Rangers in a 'sporting' sense became the standard bearer of Protestantism. Given the circumstances it was almost inevitable. However, changes in Scottish society led to the Ibrox club being demonised by many who formerly had been their 'allies'.

In the decades after World War II, the expansion of the Catholic middle class, the developing Welfare State, nationalisation, and growing secularisation were all important factors in the decrease of religious tensions in Scotland. By the 1970s it was only at Ibrox that blatant discrimination against Catholics was encouraged. Ironically, it was the churches who took it upon themselves to castigate Rangers for their policies and it was to lead to friction – most famously in 1978 when the Presbytery of Glasgow's newspaper *The Bush* publicly criticised Rangers signing policies, rebuking General Manager Willie Waddell and appealing to manager John Greig to make his views on the issue known.[18]

In the radio programme *Crossfire* months later, Rangers again came under fire from ministers, although well-known Rangers fan Reverend James Currie did defend the club.[19] The Church had made it public, they wanted nothing to do with Rangers in its present form. But if Church leaders thought criticism of Rangers would affect the situation then they were spectacularly wrong.

The bond between Rangers fans (Protestants) and the Church in the early part of the century was much stronger than latterly. From the time of the founding of Rangers (1872) up until the 1920s, the Church could materially affect the lives of its members and adherents. Church candidates representing their denominations could be found on School Boards, Parish Councils, Town Councils and County Councils.[20] Up until the 1960s the Church was closely involved with younger Protestants providing social activities like youth clubs and the Boys Brigade.[21]

However, the changes which took place in Scottish society not only affected Catholics but also lessened the presence and influence of the Protestant Churches. These changes pertained not only for Rangers fans but for Protestants as a whole. The Church lost its position as first point of contact with its members as, 'the state took greater control of people's lives' through welfare state services and the NHS. Gradually, religious influences in the public sphere decreased to the extent that, 'indirectly churches were no longer accepted as the arbiters of social policy'.[22] Also, as the churches became, 'increasingly middle class in ministry, membership and outlook, so they become even more of an irrelevance to many working class families'.[23] In addition the increasing secularisation of Scottish society, which affected all religions, further weakened the bond between the Church and its followers. Thus, in the 1970s and 80s criticism of Rangers by the Churches didn't appear to have any impact on the Ibrox fans. Their formal relationship with the Church had all but disappeared.

What of the present day relationship between Rangers fans and religion? Certainly if we take attendance figures at Church then it is clear that mainstream Protestantism has lost its grip on Scottish society. The attendances at Protestant churches plummeted in the twentieth century and the future is bleak. The Church of Scotland's absolute peak was in 1956 and the last period in Protestant church growth was between 1941 and 1956.[24] Recent figures show a downward trend in all churches in Scotland, attendance falling from 17% in 1984 to 14% of the adult population in 1994 .[25] In the last twenty years the Church of Scotland has lost around a third of its membership.[26]

Of course these figures pertain to the Protestant population as a whole and there is little evidence to assess how Rangers fans fare in this decline. But if we look at Joseph Bradley's 1990 survey of football fans we can speculate that Rangers fans are even more averse to going to Church than 'ordinary' Protestants. Only 5% claimed to attend Church every week whilst 86% claimed 'formal religious practice plays no part in their lives'.[27] For a group of people who reputedly place so much importance in religion, these are staggering figures. So do Rangers fans still consider themselves Protestants and do they see a role for the Church in their lives?

Robert Prescott

I was a Protestant by birth but I'm not any more. I'm an atheist. Religion has zero influence over me and the Protestant Churches have a rather limited role in society in general due to it not having a highly visible or recognisable leadership.

Brian Whitelaw

I consider myself a Protestant but I no longer go to Church. I was brought up in a devoutly religious family and by the time I was old enough to go my own way I had had enough of the Church and the hypocrites that populated it. I also believe you don't have to go to Church to worship.

Stephen McLeod

I am someone with an admiration of Christianity and I like to think that I have good Christian values. But does that make me a Protestant? I am struggling to answer because under the surface I am like 90% of the population who classify themselves as one thing or another for tribal labelling purposes but do nothing to actively or meaningfully demonstrate a link to any Church.

Alan McNamara

Yes, I am an Elder in the Church of Scotland. I try hard to be a good Christian, though it is not always easy. I believe in what the Lord meant to be will be. If I am unsure of anything I put my trust in him. . . The Church of Scotland's influence in Scottish society is diminishing but that effect could be halted by returning to the basic elements of Protestantism.

Peter Ewart

I am a Protestant in the sense that I was christened and confirmed as such, but I'm not church-going. Personally, I feel the Church is so far out of touch with society in general as to be laughable.

Des Ward

I no longer go to Church due to the two faced-ness of some of those who go there. . . I still believe in God and pray to him every night, and try to live a good life but apart from that, religion does not direct my life. . . The Church's influence in Scotland is far less than that of forty years ago and has next to no influence over Scottish society in general apart from maybe if you live in the Isles.

Gordon Stewart

I don't think the Church of Scotland does enough to get its point across and that's why people like me don't really follow religion.

Gordon Masterton

I am and always will be a Protestant. I feel part of a proud community and am proud of the good upbringing that the strong Protestant Wee Free faith of my family gave me. I tend to avoid going to church though, as I don't like the preachers in most churches these days.

Ian McHutchison

I was christened a Protestant but I don't go to Church any more, I don't hold it highly enough to force myself. Also it would be a little hypocritical of me as I am not sure if I even believe in what they are selling . . . Years ago the people held the Church in high esteem and would mould their views to match their Church. However, as the Church has failed to move with the times these people are seeing it for the antiquated beast that it really is.

Dugald Clark

I don't believe in God. I'm constantly amazed that religion can rule the lives of some of the

people I know. The Church doesn't affect my life at all.

Andrew Kerr

I am a Protestant and very proud of it. . . I only occasionally go to Church because I find it boring and a repackaging of what I already know.

Scott Graham

I don't go to Church any more for no good reason other than laziness. I believe in God and what the Church stands for but lack the incentive to go. Perhaps deep down I believe that since I believe in God, going to Church makes little difference.

Allan Elder

I was christened a Protestant but I don't go to Church. I don't see how anyone can go to Church and listen to what is basically a Hebrew soap opera.

Colin Glass

I'm a Protestant but I don't go to Church all that often now, because it does little for me. My wife and children go and I do think the Church is geared towards females, especially older ones, more than males. Sadly I believe the Church has lost its way and is out of touch with the needs of its members. It does still have an influence on society, although that is decreasing, but has little influence over me personally.

Dave Nichol

I was christened Church of Scotland but I don't consider myself to be anything as I don't believe in organised religion. The Church does not seem to get involved in the community. The media will always put out the views of Cardinal Winning and Tom Connelly but how many people could even name the Church of Scotland equivalents?

John Macmillan

I'm an Elder in the Church. I think more and more people, youngsters in particular, are just not going to Church and I've seen it quite frankly in my own family and it's nothing to do with being brought up that way. Both my children attended Sunday School and things like that but when they got to an age where they had their own views they decided that Church wasn't for them. . . It's partly the Church's fault because they are still a wee bit outdated. They have to get themselves modernised and do something to bring people back. But at the moment youngsters just don't seem to be interested in going. . . I think

the Church has lost a lot of influence. You hear stories of the time people were scared not to go to Church.

As far as Rangers are concerned, any link with Protestantism is a thing of the past and I think that's a major step forward. Unfortunately, It's not a thing of the past as far as a large number of supporters are concerned. People who vent their sectarian songs – they don't go to Church – so what the blazes do they know about it? It disappoints me. You hear them saying 'God Save the Queen' and such like and most of them are never inside the Church. What do they know about God?

Robert McElroy

I do go to Church, yes, but I don't go very single week and I'm not a member. I think they only have any influence over their members and activists. I don't really think they have any influence beyond that and I think even their influence over politicians is negligible. In towns and villages the Churches would have been the centre of the community but nowadays there is so much more going on like televisison which has affected many aspects of society. As people get more things to do more leisure time, more spending money and everything, the Church has become marginalised.

The relationship between the Protestant Churches and Rangers is virtually negligible, I'm sure some at Ibrox are regular attenders and they have a chaplain in David McLaggan, as James Currie was in bygone years. McLaggan is not the outgoing figure that James Currie was. I mean everyone knew James Currie, he was always at the Rangers Supporters Association's annual Rally and was guest speaker on two occasions. . . There are individual ministers who are season ticket holders at Ibrox but I don't think there was ever any close links between Rangers and any of the Protestant Churches.

John Carroll

I'm a Protestant in name only. A long absence from attending church, since Primary School, has shielded me from religious indoctrination. Therefore I could not offer an explanation as to what role or purpose Protestantism serves.

So how do modern-day Rangers fans view Catholicism?

Stephen McLeod

The Catholic Church is a very old institution which throughout its development has lost sight of the simpler message of the Bible and has become laden not only with bureaucracy and hypocrisy but also cardinal laws, none of which has its basis in the Bible. For example celibacy only became part of cardinal law in the 11th century. Most people who profess to be Catholics pay no attention whatsoever to cardinal law except when it suits them.

Kirsty Paterson

I would say Catholics are more strict and tend to force their views on others too much, for example in the issue of contraception.

Des Ward

The basic elements of Catholicism are that the Virgin

Mary is revered because she gave birth to a baby conceived in the immaculate conception. The Catholic Church also holds very antiquated views on every day topics such as the use of contraception and abortion.

Alan McNamara

I believe that it is based on error and false doctrine, ie the Pope is supposedly the supreme head of the Christian Church on earth, because they say that Peter handed down that authority to the Pope. But there is no evidence that Jesus invoked any more power to Peter than any other of his apostles. Other practices are also wrong such as confessing sins to a mere mortal and worshipping icons.

Ian McHutchison

Catholicism scares me. It demands a level of commitment and subservience which is unnatural in this day and age. It has built its strength by playing on people's fears and has got to the stage where some Catholics will make decisions which are detrimental to their own well-being in order not to incur the wrath of the Church, for example in the case of young girls who are cajoled and bribed into having children they are not ready for. Catholicism has removed self responsibility – as long as you are sorry then you are forgiven. No one, not even the church, should have the power to absolve guilt and blame. People who commit immoral acts, be they legal or illegal should bear the burden. Anything that people believe in so strongly is dangerous as it has too much influence in their lives. Nobody should rely too much on one thing, if that belief is cracked in any way then it can destroy people. . . it is this which the Catholic Church has built its wealth upon. . . we are talking about one of the richest institutions in the world, but which will see its followers starving while they collect.

Robert Prescott

Catholicism involves the more active role of the priest in the community, the power of the Pope in deciding religious policy, icon worship and a different slant in the interpretation of the role of communion.

Alistair Walker

Catholicism means basically, do what you like and all will be forgiven with a few Hail Marys.

Andrew Kerr

Catholics believe in purgatory

and spend too much time following the lead of the Pope and Mary. . . none of which is advocated by the Bible.

Colin Glass

The basic elements of Catholicism are fear, idolatry, prejudice, commercialised sin, and an obsession with sex, belief in the Virgin Mary, indoctrination, the discouragement of members to think for themselves, trans-substantiation and belief in the Pope as the Holy See.

Iain Breslin

Actually, I believe Catholics are brought up to believe they are the chosen people and are therefore better than Protestants.

NOT ONLY are Rangers fans regarded as synonymous with Protestantism, in the eyes of many Scots they are also adherents and supporters of the Orange Order. The Orange organisation is an 'ultra' Protestant body, named after Prince William of Orange who was instrumental in ensuring the future of the Protestant faith in 1690 in what is, bizarrely, perhaps the most famous event known to many Scots, the Battle of the Boyne. The Order was founded in Armagh in 1795 and its role was primarily to protect Protestants from Catholic aggression at a time of religious upheaval in Ireland.[28] Orangeism was subsequently transported from Ireland to Scotland and it was in the nineteenth century that it took root in Ayrshire, Galloway and Glasgow where the Irish Protestant immigrants settled.[29] The first 'walk' was recorded in Glasgow in 1821 and ended in a fracas with local Catholics which the police had to quell and which upset people going about their daily business. More trouble followed in the following year's parade and eventually a ban was imposed by city magistrates.[30] It is this antagonistic image of Orangeism which has lasted until the present day.

As the economic base of Scotland changed so did the make-up of the Orangemen. It was in the Protestant strongholds of the textile industries that Orangeism took root and subsequently, in the heavy industries like shipyards, steel and mining, the Orange Lodges blossomed. Over time, Scottish Protestants also became involved in Orangeism and 'by the late nineteenth century membership of an Orange Lodge had become a family tradition in many working class communitites'.[31]

However, important differences developed between the Orange Order in Ireland and its Scottish counterpart. The Order never became the force it did in Northern Ireland. Bill Murray notes, 'the Order was never received formally into the establishment the way it was in Ulster, where membership of the Lodge was a prerequisite to political power'.[32] Certainly, the Order was not able and is not able to greatly influence its members in terms of their voting patterns and membership of the Orange Order would be tantmount to political suicide for any potential Scottish politician. Neither did the Orange Lodge ever gain power and influence in the Scottish churches – 'the Presbyterian ministers who are Orangemen have never been more than a small minority of the Church of Scotland ministers'.[33]

Indeed, the Orange order has suffered a decline in membership over the years. Being very much a working class organisation it suffered with the loss of the traditional working class industries. There are varying figures on recent membership numbers but 50,000 may be the most accurate judgement which includes male and female adult members, juveniles and juniors.[34] (There are no figures as to how many of the Lodge members are Rangers fans but it would hardly be wild speculation to claim that the vast majority are at least passive supporters.)

There is no doubt that the Order's influence, credibility and respectability are at an all-time low. The Orange Lodge is not seen as one of the most progressive organisations in Scotland, often linked to the troubles in Northern Ireland and the media, 'tend to concentrate only on the nastier elements of the institution, stereotyping its members as irrational, drunken and often violent bigots'.[35] The Orange institution's figureheads and leaders have struggled to gain respect in the higher echelons of Scottish society and 'most upper and middle class Scots treat the Order with a certain snobbish disdain'.[36] The fact that the Orangemen continually struggle to get Church ministers to conduct sevices is a sign of the disapproval felt towards them.[37]

However, in the past Rangers FC openly encouraged the relationship between themselves and the Orangemen. In Glasgow in 1914, the institution was helped by the Ibrox club when Rangers and Partick Thistle played a benefit game to raise funds for the Grand Orange hall.[38] It was also known for the club to offer Ibrox stadium to the Grand Lodge of Scotland for an Orange service.[39] And there was nothing untoward when a Rangers director, James Bowie, travelled to Ulster for an Orange Order social gathering. The team itself played in Belfast on several occasions before the 1960s and in 1955 a benefit match was arranged to raise funds for an Orange hall.[40]

These examples of mutual friendship between club(s) and the Orange Order seem quite incredible when looking back from the vantage point of present day Scottish society. It is difficult to envisage any circumstances in which Rangers or any another Scottish club would play a match to raise funds for the Orange Order. In fact, Rangers FC, since the arrival of David Murray have attempted to cut all links with the Orange movement. In trying to appeal to a worldwide audience Murray has attempted to distance the club from any religious ties. This has led to criticism especially from fans in Northern Ireland who have not seen the club play a friendly match or benefit game in the province since the early eighties.

A relationship of sorts has clearly existed over many years between Rangers FC, their fans and the Orange Order. In more recent times the club has scorned their Orange image. But how successful has it been? What do modern Rangers fans think of the whole issue of the Orange Order, Rangers Football Club and Scottish society?

Peter Ewart

I'm not a member of the Orange Order but I know people who are and I've witnessed many an Orange Parade. They give the impression of being an ageing organisation and that's certainly true with regards the hierarchy. The Orange Order are unfortunately a bit of a PR nightmare, you just have to look at Drumcree. They come across as being incredibly dogmatic, which to an extent they are, but they could do a damn sight better in their handling of such situations.

Richard Pollock

I think it's just a lot of people who should just grow up. I'm not big on the Orange Lodge at all. I was brought up in Royston which nearly made me join when I was sixteen as a protest to all the shit I took, but I thought it would be daft to do it just because of that. I've never even thought about it since.

Iain Breslin

I think the majority of the Scottish population regard them as old-fashioned, single-minded bigots.

Scott Graham

I'm not a member but I've no problem with anyone who wanted to join. Although I understand the history of the Order and appreciate that it wants to remember and celebrate its history, I think it's important that it compromises on some of its marching routes, especially in Northern Ireland where there is so much tension. A lot of people hate the Orange Order because they think its only purpose is to cause trouble. Perhaps this is down to some of its members. I'm not sure.

Graham Donaldson

My perceptions of the Orange people are of an organisation unable to be separated from its twelfth of July parades and associated drunkenness and rowdyism, which spoils the celebration and message.

Tom Plunkett

Yes, I am an Orangeman and see its role as promotion of the Protestant faith, maintenance of the Monarchy in the Protestant faith and fighting within the law to allow Northern Ireland a right to self determination. Unfortunately, we have some unsavoury characters in the Order and many in Scotland tend to lump us all together with these people. We also have some of the finest men and women I have met. It has been a long time since we have had the like of the Duke of Cumberland or the Duke of Gordon in our Association but our principles are still the same and we are not going to go away. The Order was quite influential in Scotland at one time and was affiliated to some degree to the Conservative party, but we are an order of free thinkers and allow our members to vote as their conscience dictates.

Robert Prescott

My view? A secret group of closed-minded ignorants who hide behind a cloak of religious order, as they would call it, to ensure that five hundred years of sectarian hatred and conflict shall go on for five hundred more. I think the rest of Scotland mostly views them with apathy.

Brian Whitelaw

No, I'm not a member and I don't see a role for them. They are an outdated society. I'm not against societies as such, I'm a Freemason, but I'm opposed to societies who have no place in today's world. The KKK and the Orange Lodge are two such societies. I think the Protestants in the West of Scotland think there is still value to it although I believe the younger generations do not have as much interest in it. The rest of Scotland probably don't care much.

Angelique Shield

I'm a member of the Eastern Star and my view is to live and let live. Scotland has the view that because you are a member of the Lodge you are sectarian and completely against Catholics and everything they stand for but this is not the case. My uncle is a Grand Master, my dad is a past Master, all my four brothers are Masons and members of the Orange Lodge.

This is because they have family values and are willing to help anyone in need, not because they are bitter Protestants.

Stephen McLeod

I think the violence that happened at major events like Drumcree has turned public perception of Orangemen to an all time low. The true Order is a tremendously positive expression of cultural identity as anyone who has seen a parade should be able to see, but unfortunately it is sometimes hijacked as a platform for expressing hatred. Most of Scotland, outside the West, probably view it with something of a cross between indifference and distaste.

Alan McNamara

Yes, I am a member of the Orange Lodge which I see as a safeguard for the Protestant religion. We are viewed in many different ways. I have members of my own Church who openly oppose us in everything we do. Others are partly secure in the knowledge that we are here.

Des Ward

I fully believe that the Orange Order is a peaceful organisation that has been hijacked by a minority of militant idiots that turn up throughout Northern Ireland. Sinn Fein/IRA have done an excellent a job of discrediting the Order as their idiots inside have done by rising to the bait.

Andrew Kerr

Yes, I am an Orangeman. We must maintain the battle against the evil powers of Catholicism sweeping the world. The Order is viewed as sectarian. It is not. It is purely a religious order. We do not hate Catholic people, just Catholicism and its evil perpetrators.

Dougie Patterson

I see it as an outdated organisation which has no role in the modern society. With all that is being attempted in Northern Ireland, all these organisations from both persuasions have to open their eyes to the real world.

Colin Glass

In Scotland, as far as I'm concerned, the Orange Order is basically a working class movement comprising of Protestants who wish to express their faith in a colourful and musical fashion. I think they understandably suffer from a siege mentality, but they have the same right to demonstrate as anyone else in a democracy. Some of the people who attend the 'Walks', not the members, are bad news, and often bring the whole parade into disrepute. Non-Catholics generally disapprove of the Orange Order largely down to their lack of understanding of it, whilst many Catholics hate it because it stands for religious liberty which they themselves don't enjoy.

Jim Black

I no longer have any dealings with the Orange Order due to them not liking the religion of the girl I was going to marry and am still married to twenty six years down the road.

Allan Elder

My perceptions of the Orange Lodge is that of a group with a dwindling support and member-ship, who are fading over time and which have not the slightest influence in Scottish society. Public opinion is against them, and behaviour such as that displayed at Drumcree won't help them.

Robert McElroy

I'm not a member. They have a very poor PR, they are in need of a couple of spin doctors and PR people. It's difficult to say what influence they have. It may be linked to the declining influence of the churches.

John Macmillan

I'm just not interested in them. I'm sure there are many members who are good people, unfortunately they seem to attract an equal number who are maybe there for the purpose of causing havoc or whatever. I've never been a member and have no desire to be a member.

APART FROM a few who slipped the net, Rangers' anti-Catholic stance in terms of their playing staff was rock solid from around the time of the World War I up until the arrival of Maurice Johnston in 1989. Again we have to recognise the anti-Catholic strain in Scottish society, implicit or explicit, which allowed this to happen. Jamieson correctly notes that for a large part of the twentieth century the Ibrox club's sectarian practices were carried out without any interference from the major Scottish institutions such as the STUC, the major political parties or the leading Churches.[41]

Rangers FC hid behind their traditional wall of silence and Chairmen and directors, helped by a complicit Scottish society, simply refused to acknowledge the issue. But there were several 'slip ups' which gave the game away. In 1967 vice Chairman Matt Taylor claimed the Rangers refusal to sign Catholics was 'part of their tradition'.[42] In 1969 chairman John Lawrence said the non-Catholic policy had, 'been with the club since it was formed'.[43] Both men displayed an appalling ignorance of the club's origins. Gradually, the practice which dared not speak its name was challenged. But Willie Waddell, when club chairman in 1972, assured the waiting world that Rangers were not sectarian, only to backtrack in the aftermath of a riot at Aston Villa in 1976. Stung by accusations that the misbehaviour of the fans was the manifestation of endemic Ibrox bigotry, Waddell said Rangers would, 'in future sign a Catholic if one good enough came along'.[44] Given the low calibre of player who often filled blue jerseys in the following decade, it was clearly an empty promise. Not that some fans were bothered.

Many people will remember the television footage of Andy Cameron, the celebrity Rangers fan, bravely speaking after a Rangers AGM of his desire to see the Ibrox club sign Catholic players. He was berated by several angry fans who told him they considered Catholics to be, by definition, inferior. It was an embarassing episode which did nothing to improve the perception of Rangers supporters amongst the general public.

In hindsight the club officials who denied the existence of the sectarian practice perhaps, in some misguided way, thought that they were somehow protecting the 'good name' of the club. But there was no doubt an arrogance infused Ibrox, a feeling of invincibilty and of being above criticism. Whilst all of Scotland knew about Rangers' no-Catholic practice, not least Rangers fans, many of whom openly endorsed it, Rangers FC stuck its head in the sand.

29

Alan McNamara

Yes, Rangers operated a policy of not signing RCs. But my view is the same as that taken by the Roman Catholic Church when it comes to its schools and teachers. It's the freedom to choose who you employ. I believe there was a strong relationship between the club and Protestantism at one time but that is no longer there, although it has been carried on by the fans.

Colin Glass

Perhaps there was a sectarian employment policy but not to the extent that the media suggests. I personally worked full time for Rangers Pools for four years in the mid seventies and it was never an issue. Catholics were employed right up to a senior level.

Dave Nichol

As far as the playing staff were concerned then yes, Rangers did operate a sectarian policy. It was a shameful policy but it is definitely over. Rangers owe a lot to Souness, Holmes and Mo Johnston.

Charlie McIntyre

You'd have to say they did discriminate pre-Maurice Johnston. At the time you had guys running the club who were traditionalists, who were brought up that way but times change and when Souness came in, who was obviously married to a Catholic, then things changed quicker than we probably all thought. But it changed for the better.

Iain Breslin

The Rangers/Protestant thing is a tradition that is beginning to run its course. There is no signing 'policy', except on the basis of talent and the captain is an Italian Catholic, which is a good thing.

Richard Pollock

There's no doubt Rangers had sectarian signing policies and there's also no doubt that it held the club back.

Peter Ewart

Rangers will always attract the Protestants and Celtic will always attract Catholics. Both clubs are held in their respective communities as symbols of what they stand for and it simply doesn't matter that we are signing Catholics.

Des Ward

Of course Rangers have operated a sectarian signing policy in the past. I certainly feel this was and is wrong and if you want to be successful then you must look at the abilities of a player.

David Taylor

For years Rangers used to sign only Protestants but I feel this hindered our progress. Players with great abilities could not be signed because of their beliefs.

Ian McHutchison

No one can deny the links Rangers had with Protestantism, why should we? Rangers are a Protestant Club like Celtic is Catholic. You cannot deny your history. In a time when religion was an integral part in people's lives, Rangers and Celtic grew and prospered by building on their links with religion and playing on their rivalry. I think we can say Rangers are still the Protestant club in Scotland although they will happily employ Catholics, Hindus, Jews or whatever.

Alistair Walker

It was outrageous that Rangers used to choose players based purely on their religion rather than their footballing ability. The Protestant thing, if it exists, is fairly superficial. I would be interested to know how many of the numbers who attend the game on a Saturday, attend the Church on a Sunday.

Graham Donaldson

I had no problems with Rangers' Protestant-only policies. The people in charge saw it as right for the times. Certain bowling clubs, pubs and the like had the same membership and so Rangers were just in keeping with other establishments of the time. This policy should be viewed in the light of a similar one in many walks of life by followers of Catholicism . . . many supporters still have strong Protestant beliefs but the club has moved on from this.

Scott Graham

Yes, I accept accusations of Rangers once operating a sectarian signing policy are true. I am simply glad it has ended. If Rangers had said in the past that they would not sign blacks, Jews or Hindus then they would have been correctly despised, yet people seemed to accept the exclusion of Catholics.

Allan Elder

Rangers operated their signing policies for historical reasons. I view this as a mistake in Rangers past which cost them dearly on the pitch and allowed Celtic nine championships in a row. I would love to know what would have happened in that era had the people in charge at Ibrox been as forward thinking as those in charge now. The club appears to be trying to distance themselves from the idea of being predominantly Protestant through signing players based purely on ability. Some of the fans, however, have still to make that move.

Robert Prescott

There is no question Rangers had a policy of not signing Catholics and I'm absolutely disgusted by it as it gave solidity to religious sectarianism.

Brian Whitelaw

Rangers obviously have Protestant connections and groundings but the vast majority of fans attending games do not go to Church and would be challenged to tell you the name of more than five books in the Bible. Also many profess to be atheists whilst defending their Protestant faith. Mind boggling.

Stephen McLeod

It's a point of fact that Rangers and Protestantism are related. I am sure that Rangers encouraged this association for many years and I'm annoyed that Rangers today cannot openly admit this part of their history because it is nothing to be

ashamed of. It was simply a reflection of the society we lived in at the time.

Jim Black

Rangers have always been and will always be, in my eyes, a Protestant team supported by Protestants. Yes, for years they operated a sectarian employment policy and had a great deal of success. It was great while we were able to do this but like all walks of life things have to change.

Tom Plunkett

I think it's great that we are associated with the religion of the land. There is nothing wrong with being a Protestant club in a Protestant land. I agreed with the no-Catholic policy of old, as I believe it is not a right to play for Rangers but an honour. But if we want to attain any great heights in Europe, then we must sign the best players available. This does not mean that we deviate from our Protestant background, as this is what made us what we are, and we should never forget it.

AS A CONSEQUENCE of their signing policies Rangers fans have been criticised for being more anti-Catholic than pro-Protestant. Is this criticism valid?

Iain Breslin

I think it's more of a case of being anti-IRA and anti-Celtic. These two things do have an association with Catholics, so perhaps this is where the idea comes from. When you have 50,000 fans signing the praises of a Roman Catholic Rangers captain then how can fans be anti-Catholic?

Dave Taylor

Sadly it is probably true that we are more anti-Catholic than pro-Protestant. Many of the fans signing the songs have no idea what they are signing about and have probably never set foot in a Church.

Ian McHutchison

Rangers fans are anti-Celtic who happen to be Catholic. You get at your rivals any way you can.

Scott Graham

It's probably true that Rangers fans are more anti-Catholic than pro-Protestant. After all they don't sing hymns or praise God, but they do sing anti-Fenian songs, although technically Fenians aren't Roman Catholics. It's another example of a lack of education.

Brian Whitelaw

I agree with that sentiment absolutely. As I've said, many of us do not practise any kind of faith or religion whatsoever.

Des Ward

It is much easier to hate something than understand it and there is a sizeable amount of Rangers and Celtic fans who bitterly hate the other without being truly understanding of Protestantism or Catholicism.

Gordon Masterton

I don't think Rangers fans are anti-Catholic, I think they are anti-Fenian – in the true sense of the word.

THE ENDING of Rangers sectarian signing practice curiously provoked more vexation at Celtic Park than at Ibrox. When Maurice Johnston signed for Rangers in 1989 the hatred poured on him by the Parkhead faithful was fierce in its intensity and he was, and still is, castigated as a 'Judas'. Ostensibly, the Celtic fans claimed they were betrayed by the Nantes striker who had originally pledged his future to his former club. But there would surely have been little fuss if Johnston had signed for any team other than Rangers. Underpinning the vitriol was the realisation that no longer could Celtic fans pontificate about the sectarian character of the Ibrox club.

Celtic fans had complained, quite rightly and with good reason, of bias against Catholics in institutions and workplaces all over Scotland. Gradually, discrimination on grounds of religion was ended and only Ibrox stood as an obtrusive reminder of a by-gone age. However, when the last bastion of Scottish Protestant sectarianism was breached, Catholic Johnston, however weak his faith was, was condemned. He had let the side down. The old chicken and egg joke re-emerged in a new format. Why would Johnston want to sign for Rangers – they didn't sign Catholics!?

Previous Ibrox boards, who had feared that signing a Catholic would result in their fan base disappearing, were proved wrong. If they had taken the time and energy to canvass the Ibrox support on the issue they would have known their fears were unfounded. A few 'die hards' did emerge before the television cameras to renounce their Ibrox connections but these were isolated and often stage-managed incidents. It had been a gross insult to all Rangers fans to consider them so biased that they would stop supporting their team if it contained Catholics. The controversial signing signalled the beginning of a trend and in recent years Rangers have pursued a signing policy most clubs employ – recruit the best players they can afford. Almost by definition, some of the many overseas players who have come to Ibrox have been Catholics and one of the most popular in recent times has been Jorg Albertz, 'The Hammer'. Rangers have also recruited Catholics from within Scotland and Neil McCann (Celtic fans also consider him a 'Judas') arrived at Ibrox and settled in well with no adverse reaction from the Rangers supporters. Amaruso and McCann have been criticised in recent times for loss of form or for individual errors during games, but their religion has not been questioned from the stands. What do the fans think of the club's present signing policy?

Scott Graham

I don't care about Catholics in the Rangers team as long as they are good enough. Unfortunately, I don't think it will make a lot of difference to the moronic element who attach themselves to Rangers FC.

Charlie McIntyre

When Johnston came I had mixed feelings to be honest. On the one hand I was disappointed that traditions were gone. I was proud Rangers were a Protestant team but when I look back I'm a wee bit embarrassed about that. On the other hand, he was one of the best strikers in Europe at the time and it was a major slap in the face for Celtic. Nowadays, I haven't a problem with the situation

Robert Prescott

It is an irrelevance even if there is a predominance of Catholics in the team. It is simply a matter of picking the best players regardless of religious make-up. I hope it will have some positive long term effects on the fans, but I doubt if it will do much to reduce sectarianism as the problem goes far deeper than Catholics in blue shirts.

Alan Park

To begin with I wasn't happy with this new policy. I had to bite the bullet. It's a policy now of getting a team together regardless of religion which I'm all for. I know a manager in my work who has never been back to Ibrox since Rangers signed Johnston and there's a couple on my bus who wished they could go back to only signing Protestants.

Kirsty Paterson

To be perfectly honest, it doesn't bother me one way or the other. As long as the player pulling on the Rangers jersey is giving their all for that shirt, they could be alien as far as I'm concerned. I think however, that there are some fans who would have totally different views on this.

Brian Whitelaw

I couldn't give a monkeys what religion or colour Rangers players are, and that's being honest. I think most Rangers fans think along the same lines. They want success for the club, that's all.

Stephen McLeod

The old days have gone for good. I have no problems with Catholics in the team and indeed I thoroughly enjoyed watching us beat Celtic 4-2 the other week with a bunch of RCs in the team.

Alan McNamara

I hated the day Mo Johnston signed because he pretended to be a Catholic. I have no objection to anyone who wishes to practise their faith – indeed I am one of Amaruso's biggest fans – but I have no wish to see another of the Mo Johnston ilk at Ibrox.

Allan McEwan

I can sit on the bus today and listen to people say 'I'm glad we got rid of that wee so and so' but I never heard anyone shouting at the time. I just want to see Rangers winning. We probably done ourselves more harm than anything else over the years. I think it had a lot to do with tradition at Ibrox through Struth and Symon – they installed tradition and their tradition was, 'We are the people'. It wasn't restricted to Rangers. I work in a stockbrokers and it was the same there up until a few years ago. We had to get away from it all and we've won more trophies than any time in our history since then.

Colin Glass

I personally welcomed the signing of Maurice Johnston for Rangers in 1989 and it was proved that the real bigots were the Celtic fans who behaved so disgracefully over the signing. The vast bulk of Rangers fans welcomed him. It was the Celtic support who were spouting forth their sectarian bile at the time and even Ernie Walker, the SFA secretary, criticised it. It was a spectacular gesture and it was ironic that those who had criticised the club for not signing Catholics did not praise them when they did do so. . . so Catholics in the team is not an issue with me at all.

Dave Nichol

I couldn't even tell you who is what religion at Ibrox. I would guess the Italians are Catholics. Having said that the papers were compelled to tell us McCann was a Catholic when he signed. It may mean that eventually more Catholics will support the team.

Jim Black

I am not over the moon about all the Catholics at Ibrox but as long as they perform for the club I stand by what is needed to make the club successful, especially in Europe.

Craig Knox

I'm delighted with Rangers signing anybody they want. Look at Neil McCann – two goals at Celtic Park to win the League, that's him an instant hero. It's good that guys want to come and play for Rangers. We missed out on good players because of the old sectarian

policy – it did go against us. There's about six of the Rangers team just now who are Catholic and there's no problems.

Des Ward

I really couldn't care if we had a team full of black Catholics, as long as we were winning and had the future set out to nurture better Scottish players to come through. Although Rangers are a Scottish team, I feel that realism must prevail and foreigners of different cultures and religions are going to come in.

Ian McHutchison

As soon as they sign for Rangers they become part of the family. Ninety percent of Rangers fans feel they same, otherwise they wouldn't pack out Ibrox every other week.

John Macmillan

I think the club took the right and the only step they could take in today's world, to try and seperate themselves from that. That doesn't mean to say you can't be proud to be a Protestant or you can't be proud to be a Roman Catholic, a Jew or whatever – to each their own – but the club will not take the step back. Unfortunately, some supporters still have that blinkered view and that will probably continue throughout my lifetime. In saying that, nowadays I think the majority of the support are more concerned with trying to win trophies rather than what religion players are and that's a very positive step as far as I'm concerned.

John Carroll

As a Rangers supporter I only want us to buy the best players possible, irrespective of their religion. Rangers fans should get used to good players playing for the club, whoever they are.

Robert McElroy

I was in favour of signing Catholics. I think there would be few who would disagree. I think it was a case of signing the right man at the right time. After signing such a person as Maurice Johnston which stunned Scotland and the Celtic supporters, everything else became almost secondary.

Garry Lynch

I don't support Rangers because they are, or rather were, a Protestant insitution. I want eleven winners rather than eleven Protestant losers. We don't know what half the team are and we don't care, and just about everybody who goes to Ibrox now feels the same.

ALTHOUGH RANGERS now sign Catholic players, their critics maintain a sectarian residue remains within the Ibrox support and is demonstrated in the songs and chants heard at matches. Some of the criticism has emanated from within the club itself.

David Murray is the first chairman of Rangers to vociferously and continually criticise the fans for the songs they sing. He has claimed that whilst watching games he 'cringes' when he hears some of the songs: 'I just don't see why people feel the need to sing songs like 'Are you watching fenian scum', It's unacceptable. . . Surely our fans can celebrate our success without denigrating the club like this. We are a European club in the true sense of the word and we have to prove it'.[45]

Given that during most league matches at Ibrox nowadays

there is very little singing, it is the fans who follow Rangers away from home, the ones who see themselves as more 'loyal', who stand accused by the Rangers chairman amongst others. At these games you can hear Orange songs and cruder versions of standard Rangers songs such as 'Follow Follow' sung with gusto. A section of the Ibrox fans broker no criticism whatsoever and there is no doubt that the songs are now sung in a defiant manner, some fans almost revelling in the disdain they inspire. Are the criticisms of the songs Rangers fans sing valid?

Andrew Kerr

Chants are traditional and most fans get a buzz from singing them. They don't do any harm. I think David Murray is right to cut out the swearing but not to change the songs completely.

Colin Glass

David Murray should stop apologising for who we are. Some of the songs go a bit far but why should Rangers fans stop singing 'The Sash' just to please opposition fans? The main ones who are offended are the very ones who sing pro-IRA songs and find the flag of our country provocative. Murray's finger is not on the pulse of the Rangers fans. . . Is 'Flower of Scotland' not racist or offensive also?

Dave Taylor

I don't have a problem with the 'FTP' chants because I am genuinely opposed to him and his beliefs although chants at a football match may not be the most eloquent way of illustrating this. I am very happy to sing *The Sash* which is a folk song and less militaristic than *Flower of Scotland*. I think David Murray is trying to appease the media and many fans find that offensive. You cannot sanitise football fans.

Peter Ewart

David Murray's criticism of sectarian chants is up to him, he's entitled to his opinion. Personally, and I know I speak for a lot of Northern Ireland Bears here, an Old Firm game is an excellent semi-controlled environment to offload pent up anger, better in song than in action. Those who are well enough informed to take offence at such songs are not the innocent parties they make themselves out to be. If being anti-IRA, anti-Sinn Fein and anti-United Ireland makes me a bigot, well that's up to others to judge.

Kirsty Paterson

I don't think they are something that will ever completely disappear. I also don't think in general that they are meant in the context in which a lot of the media portray them. It's part of the emotion of Ibrox and it's something that's very difficult not to be swept up in.

Gordon Stewart

I don't feel the sectarian songs mean very much to most people who sing them. Nobody will hear these songs and go out and kill a Catholic. I think that most Rangers and Celtic fans sing these songs to be traditional and don't believe in what they are singing. I feel David Murray should appeal through the supporters clubs if he wants people to stop the singing of these songs. Going to the media is useless as Rangers fans don't listen to the media any more.

Tom Plunkett

It depends what you call sectarian. Some of our songs have an Ulster theme which I do not believe to be sectarian. I do however, believe that those who chant FTP after our songs should stop immediately. It has no place at Ibrox. Murray was criticising the song 'Are you watching Fenian Scum'. The term Fenian is self-imposed and thus can't be insulting to Celtic fans and the term scum can't be regarded as sectarian. Therefore, when Celtic supporters continue to align themselves with that murderous shower, they should have no complaints.

Wull McLay

We'll sing them till the day we die, to do anything other would be rank hypocrisy. The club got very rich on its policy and we are a product of that policy. It will become diluted in time but not for a very very long time and I don't have a problem with moving forward.

Alan Park

I think Murray should just shut his mouth. Rangers fans should be allowed to sing what they want. They're not going to stop because he moans about it. We're paying good money, we should be able to do what we want. He should keep these things to himself and not go public saying he's upset about it.

Dougie Patterson

It will take a long time to change. For all the press coverage, Bhoys against Bigotry still does not stop the pro-IRA chants. People need to be realistic about the West of Scotland and how hard it will be to change years of this nonsense.

Jim Black

Murray must have heard these songs long before he invested in the club and must have known that they will not go away just because he says he doesn't like them. I have to admit we are ruining some of our better ones by adding silly bits to them, like in the case of 'Simply the Best'.

Ian McHutchison

Murray should shut his cake-hole. Rangers fans have made him extraordinarily wealthy. He bought that club for what? About ten million? And now his stake is close to around two hundred million. We are the club, he is the caretaker. If he doesn't like what we sing he can get out. When Scotland play we hear 'Flower of Scotland' which is all about fighting and killing Englishmen, yet nobody bats an eyelid because they know we

don't really want to kill the English. Rangers fans don't want to slaughter Catholics, they want to sing songs to encourage their team. Murray has helped destroy the atmosphere at Ibrox, guys being evicted for singing songs they have been singing for years. This man should be standing up for us. Without us there is no Rangers and he shouldn't forget this.

Fiona Kell

I am pretty indifferent about this because I don't think they are as bad as they seem. Rangers fans have been singing these songs for years and the majority of them probably have Catholics as their best friends. Murray has been criticising the fans because the newspapers are criticising him and the club.

Dugald Clark

David Murray has a point about these songs. The club is no longer solely a Protestant environment. The chants and views of some of the fans are quite archaic.

Allan McEwan

People sing songs at Rangers matches and they're singing songs that they've sung for years. The songs are almost irrelevant – you're trying to create a noise and an atmosphere around the stadium. It's part of becoming a Rangers fan that you learn these songs. It's almost as if we go overboard because of the Protestant aspect of Rangers. I think David Murray should just let it go. He's wrong to criticise Rangers fans for singing 'Rule Britannia' or 'God save the Queen'. Don't try and tell me that during an Old Firm game at Ibrox it's a minority of fans singing these songs. You go to Parkhead and they've got four guys on the screens singing 'Fields of Athenrye'. I think Celtic get away it.

Richard Pollock

I'll sing the songs but that's as far as it goes. I think David Murray is getting a wee bit carried away. It doesn't matter how many Catholics you sign, the fans are still going to sing the songs. It's not a bad thing unless it's taken to the extremes like UVF and this jargon, that's got nothing to do with Rangers. Other teams in other countries have certain traditions and histories but we're made out to be the bad guys.

Alistair Walker

These songs are as repugnant as the racist chants south of the border and are proving as difficult to eradicate. David Murray has a responsibility to try and end the cycle of hatred this generates.

Craig Knox

It works both ways. Celtic play 'Fields of Athenrye' or whatever. They say it's not sectarian but they do it just to wind the Rangers fans up. It's tradition singing these songs. I can't see it changing.

Allan Elder

I wish the sectarian chants would stop, but I believe that some of the fans that grow up in the central belt are conditioned into that. I think Murray has a right to criticise but I believe it will take someone like Amaruso or one of the other players asking for it to be stopped before real headway can be made.

Angelique Shield

No one ever brings up the songs sung at Parkhead about the IRA or killing soldiers. People should get their facts right. 'The Sash' is just about a boy who wears his father's sash.

Stephen McLeod

I think some of the songs sung are dreadful and I wish there were more alternative songs sung which concentrated on celebrating the team. For the record I don't think 'The Sash' or 'Derry's Walls' are sectarian or offensive and are popular songs from our terracing culture. However, some of 'the Pope' or UVF songs really have no place in a football stadium.

Alan McNamara

It depends on what you call sectarian chants. If you mean the references to the Pope then I agree with both the fanzines, *Follow Follow* and *Number One*, it should be dropped now. If you mean 'The Sash' or 'Derry's Walls' then they are part of our Protestant culture, just as 'The Fields of Athenrye' is part of Celtic's culture. As to the use of the word 'Fenian', well, it's the republicans who call themselves that, as in 'The bold Fenian men'. Murray should just keep quiet on the issue. You see, he cannot ask us to give the team loud vocal backing, knowing the songs we will sing and then the next day in the press criticise us.

Des Ward

The sectarian chants at the game are part of the history of the club. Ask the majority of the supporters the words to *The Sash* and the like and they'll spout it chapter and verse. Ask them the history of the songs they are singing and, especially in Scotland, they wouldn't have a clue. Ask them again if they know a Catholic and you'll find at least half will have a Catholic friend. Murray would like to live in an ideal world where no one hates each other but the chants will remain and you will always get the fans singing the songs without really understanding why they are singing them.

Gordon Masterton

I think if we drop the FTP part then the rest of the songs would be acceptable.

Charlie McIntyre

I'm there on a Saturday and I'll sing the songs the same as everyone else but when I get home I'll take one hat off and put another one on type of thing.

You seem to change on a Saturday. Most of us are not like that in real life. The majority of songs are sung to get at the other side especially at the Celtic games. It annoys them so that's why we do it. The club should do better and if they're serious they should get some songs for the fans.

John Macmillan

I support Murray's stance on the songs which are sung. Some of the words which are sung in the songs are not only anti-Catholic but they're pure filth and in my view there's no place for that in football. How can you encourage families to football? If I had any youngsters I would have second thoughts about taking them. But let me say Rangers supporters are not alone in this, you hear bad language in England and in other Scottish grounds. I've had a couple of meeting with David Murray but he's never formally come out with the Association on that issue but if he wanted to do that and make it public, I would be only too happy to assist. I don't think it's easy to get rid of these songs and I find it difficult to know what more the club can do – they've ejected fans, they've taken season tickets off them. There's a limit to what you can do. We want to go back to the days of singing the Rangers songs.

Robert McElroy

David Murray and some of the papers may be up in arms at this but I don't think it's time for a change. I don't see in all honesty anything wrong in traditional songs. What I do think is wrong – and I do emphasise this because I do differentiate between the proper singing of the songs and the variations that we sadly get all too often at Ibrox – you know the adding of foul and abusive language, I think that's entirely wrong. I certainly wouldn't condone the singing of 'Are you watching Fenian scum', 'The Sash' and songs like that. The traditional folk songs, if they are sung with the proper words, I don't think there's anything wrong with them. . . I don't think there is any hypocrisy with having Catholic players and singing 'The Sash'. . . but I think we can get too carried away with the importance of these things.

John Carroll

The sectarian chants are an embarrassment. David Murray is correct in his condemnation of the fans who sing those songs and it's particularly embarrassing when your own family are Catholics.

THE CHAPTER began by looking at the emergence and development of Rangers' Protestant identity which saw the Ibrox club championed as the sporting wing of a Scottish Protestant society. However, this is no longer the case and Protestantism, in an Ibrox context, is no longer seen in a positive light. Graham Walker of Belfast University, claims that since the sixties Rangers FC and their fans, 'Have been held up to represent the worst aspects of Protestantism – bigotry, dourness and conservatism'.[46] Certainly, in the last thirty years Rangers fans' brand of Protestantism has been closely linked to Orangeism, which in turn has been associated with the troubles in Northern Ireland from which Scottish society has been keen to keep its distance.

Of course the Protestantism of Rangers fans, however we define it, must be considered in the context of the overall Scottish Protestant community. As noted earlier, the Churches are emptying at an alarming rate and the long term future of organised religion is bleak. In 1999 only 56 candidates enrolled to be Church of Scotland ministers – down from 181 in 1992.[47] But that diminishing figure may well be enough to cater for adherents in the future if Protestants continue to turn away from formal worship. Social and cultural developments have made it is possible for nominal or notional Protestants to go through their whole lives without having any dealings with the church. And many do.

Walker claims, 'The Church has not promoted itself positively, it is split within itself as how to respond to social changes and it has become very ineffective, so the whole sense of Protestant self-confidence or the image of the Protestant community of itself is very much weaker'. In a specifically Ibrox context, there is no discernible bond between Protestant Church leaders and Rangers fans. Walker explains, 'A lot of ministers are aloof. There is undoubtedly a large section of the Kirk who would just want to wash their hands with Rangers. When I was growing up and going to Ibrox, I was aware of a great deal of disapproval about this from teachers and there was a lot of middle class Presbyterian abhorrence about Rangers'.[48]

Rangers fans and Protestant Church leaders don't have the affinity that their rivals Celtic have with 'their' Church. A telling example of the relationship between Rangers and Celtic and their respective church leaders came in a television documentary about the issue of bigotry in Scotland. Roman Catholic interviewee Bishop Devine was asked if he was a Celtic supporter? 'Of course', came the reply, as if he had been asked if he believed in God. And the Church of Scotland minister John Harvey, was he a Rangers supporter? 'No, I'm more of a rugby man', he replied, almost incredulous at the question![49]

Rangers fans clearly hold complex and sometimes contradictory religious views and attitudes which makes it very difficult to arrive at any sort of conclusion. Despite a strong claim of Protestant beliefs from the Ibrox faithful it evidently doesn't involve direct contact with the Church or its leaders. This is not a criticism in that Church attendance does not indicate moral superiority. But it must be considered a strange type of religious affiliation which involves a constant reiteration of religious identity, but doesn't involve participating in Church activities

The nature of the fans' relationship with the Orange Order also reveals complexities. Whilst there is not the explicitly strong support there perhaps once was for the ailing institution, and indeed many have renounced it, some Rangers fans seem happy to mimic the sentiments of the Order, particularly its Ulster agenda.

These sentiments perhaps impact on attitudes towards Catholicism where there is still some lingering negativity. There are no problems in most fans' minds with the signing of Catholics, indeed it is overwhelmingly encouraged, but there is a sense that Catholicism is tolerated as long as it's hidden. Certainly there is no compromise on the most complex issue – the songs and chants of the Rangers fans. The traditional songs are still sung even though Protestants are often in the minority on the Rangers team sheet.

Fans argue that simply singing Orange songs doesn't make Rangers supporters bigots any more than singing 'Flower of Scotland' makes Scots racists. It is true that football stadia have never been the most politically correct arenas. People can get caught up in the atmosphere at games but accusations of bigotry are harder to defend in the crude dirges aimed at Catholics such as 'Are you watching Fenian scum?' Walker argues that the traditional songs, if not the chants, are part of a bigger socio/political picture, the perception amongst some Protestants that they are being ignored. These grievances are particulary strong at Ibrox 'and for a lot of Rangers fans football is the only place where they can stand up and defiantly sing 'The Sash' and say, hey, I still count'.[50]

3

Rangers Fans and Politics

UNTIL SUCH TIMES as ballot papers in local and national elections allow for indicating what football team voters support, attempting to find out the exact political make-up of football fans will be a very difficult task. Particularly so in the case of Rangers supporters who are spread not only throughout Scotland but all over the world.

Some limited survey work was carried out in 1990 by Joseph Bradley of Caledonian University in Glasgow. Bradley conducted a poll of football fans in Scotland which noted their political allegiances. The survey was small in scale and it is of course now politically dated, but it noted a healthy link between Rangers fans and a Conservative party persuasion. 32% of Rangers fans voted Tory at a time when only 14-16% of the overall population did so.[1] These stronger than normal links to the Conservative party will come as no surprise to fans of other clubs in Scotland.

The view of most modern day football supporters in Scotland is that Rangers fans lie politically somewhere between Conservatism and extreme right wing. Certainly, a stranger to Scotland visiting a Rangers match would see and hear evidence which would confirm those perceptions. On sale around the ground would be merchandise with pictures of the Queen and Union flags, and as mentioned in the previous chapter, fans regularly regale whoever cares to listen with the national anthem and other songs like 'Rule Britannia' and 'No surrender to the IRA'. On the odd occasion they might also witness the National Front or similar groups attempting to sell their wares with a view to recruitment.

The Ibrox (and thus Protestant) link with Conservatism is longstanding. David McCrone neatly sums up the affinity Protestants developed with the Conservative party in the latter part of the nineteenth and the early part of the twentieth century. He notes that religion had always played an important part in politics in Scotland. The dual Conservative/ Protestant identity,

> 'consisted of a complex inter related elements of Protestantism and Unionism welded together by a strong sense of British national and imperial identity, and symbolised by the Union Jack. This version of Scottishness was not at odds with Conservative rhetoric about British national and Imperial identity, given the powerful strand of militarism which ran through Scottish society in the late nineteenth and early twentieth centuries.'[2]

If McCrone highlights the positive aspects of the dual identity then Graham Walker identifies the negative, sectarian element in politics which was also influential in shaping allegiances, arguing that, 'the Unionist party, especially in the interwar period, gave overt political expression to the fears and prejudices of many Protestant Scots. Anti-Catholicism functioned as an important if negative expression of Protestant identity.'[3]

Thus, it was 'normal' for many working class Protestants

to vote for the Unionists (which the Conservatives were called until 1965) and from the 1920s to the 1960s, 'Conservative support in Scotland was normally equal to Labour's and often greater. In 1955 for example the Conservatives had 50% of the vote and more than 50% of the seats'.[4]

Obviously all Protestants were not Rangers fans but it would not be too speculative to claim that many Rangers fans fitted all too neatly into the working class Tory model. And despite the collapse of the Tory party in Scotland in recent years, which has seen them marginalised, if not demonised, Ibrox support for Conservatism remains.

Ferrier and McElroy in their comprehensive book *Rangers: The Complete Record*, claim that Rangers are 'the flag carrier of what the majority of Scots would consider to be national virtues – Protestant, Monarchist tradition and Unionist'.[5] Sandy Jamieson compounds the Conservative credentials of the Ibrox club in his book on former player-manager Graeme Souness. Jamieson links Souness and Rangers FC with the Thatcherist values of the 1980s, and notes that, 'even the diehards were surprised by the way Souness demonstrated his own belief in the Union by importing two of the Queen's finest Englishmen (Chris Woods and Terry Butcher) into the defence of the faith'.[6]

The official club publications – the matchday programme, weekly newspaper and monthly magazine – mention almost nothing about Rangers in political terms which is understandable given their football-only remit of features, pictures and competitions. However, the unofficial publications, the fanzines, which purport to be the voice of the true fans, buck the normal fanzine trend in that they are right wing in editorial terms and have regular, if sporadic, articles and comments of a political nature which tend to support the editorial agenda.

The *Rangers Historian*, written by Robert McElroy, a member of the Conservative party, clearly continues the right wing agenda of the author. One issue commented on the 'Unionist traditions of our team' and claimed that during a trip to Ireland, Rangers and their followers were perceived as the 'Unionist enemy'.[7]

McElroy, author of several books on Rangers, is candid about his political leanings. 'I consider myself British, I'm a Unionist. For example, at the Scotland-England games in November, I would have stood for 'God Save the Queen', I wouldn't have stood for 'Flower of Scotland'. . . I was a keen supporter of Margaret Thatcher. My opinion is she's the finest Prime Minister of this century, without question. I resigned from the Conservative party, although I still voted Tory, when she was deposed. I didn't have anything to do with them for seven or eight years thereafter. In my opinion she could still be Prime Minister today. I don't think the Conservative party would be in the state they are in, had she retained her leadership'.[8]

The *Number One* fanzine is humour-based and does not feature politics to any great extent. Its editor, 'The Entertaining Apprentice', admits however, that, 'The overall thrust of the views in the fanzine would head in the direction of loyalist/ unionist'.[9] Contributors include 'The Hamilton Loyalist' who asked, 'What's the problem with 'Rule Britannia', 'God Save the Queen' and 'No Surrender'?'[10] However, the editor qualifies his assertion of a right wing bias in the publication by claiming that, 'We don't intentionally print the one viewpoint, it's just that the SNP and the left of centre fans can't be bothered to write in'.

The *Follow Follow* fanzine has a clear right wing agenda. Its more recent dalliance with politics include selling trinkets for the Scottish Unionist party, a political group set up in the 1980s and which mainly targets disaffected Tories in Scotland. And if the discerning fan wants T-shirts with 'No Surrender' emblazoned upon them, they can find them within the pages of *Follow Follow*.[11] One contributor, 'The Fox', wrote of Rangers as 'Protestant Unionist Scots' and feared that in a politically correct Britain, 'Rangers will have no Union Jack, no national anthem, no 'Rule Britannia'. . .'[12]

But it would be wrong to claim that politics dominates any of the unofficial publications, which in the main concentrate on more typical fanzine concerns such as ticket prices, team selections and media coverage.

Throughout the century there has been support from within the club for right of centre political parties and policies going back to John Ure Primrose who was the Rangers chairman and a Liberal Unionist MP, right up to the present-day Chairman David Murray who makes no secret of his Conservative sympathies. Former vice-chairman Donald Findlay was a leading figure in the 'No-No' campaign in the 1999 referendum for a Scottish Parliament and is one of the most prominent Conservative figures in Scotland.[13]

High profile players and staff like Terry Butcher and Walter Smith have also nailed their colours firmly to the Conservative mast in recent years at a time when the Tories in Scotland have been deeply unpopular. And at the height of anti-Thatcher sentiment in Scotland in 1991, the club invited the Prime Minister along to Ibrox giving critics of Rangers another reason to castigate the club.

What of the club's supporters? Are they influenced by their heroes at Ibrox in terms of how they vote or what political views they hold?

Allan Elder

I've never regarded my support for Rangers as having anything to do with politics or religion. And I wouldn't be influenced by any personality in terms of voting. I would always trust my own instincts and opinions.

Charlie McIntyre

Donald Findlay? I would talk to him about Rangers but when it came to politics I would say I have a different opinion completely and let's leave it at that. I think there is a lot of blind faith with some Rangers fans and because of David Murray we're perceived as a Tory club, with 'God save the Queen' and 'Rule Britannia'. A lot of Rangers fans will vote for the Tories just because Rangers are associated with them. Some of the guys I know love Rangers that much that if Murray came out and said 'I'm going to vote SNP at the next election', they would go with him.

Angelique Shield

My influences are not because of the team I support. Politics is a very different ball game. I normally vote for the party I think have the best policies at the time and I have never been influenced by anyone. I suit myself.

Colin Glass

No, I don't want or need football people, especially wealthy ones, telling me how to vote. I can make up my own mind.

Dougie Brown

Sometimes I think it shows how out of touch with the supporters those people are at Ibrox. Margaret Thatcher and her cronies decimated Scotland with their policies and attitude and some players and management come out in support for them! I mean, I can see the point of Murray and Findlay – the Tories have been good to people like them – but they don't live in the same world as most of the Rangers fans. Then again having Findlay on their side has probably backfired on the Tories. No, I don't listen to them trying to push the Tory vote up.

Graham Gardner

I keep my politics and football completely separate. I know some Rangers fans who are staunch Tories because of their links with Rangers and Protestantism but I'm not one of them.

Jim Black

I'm aware of Rangers links with the Conservatives but I take no notice. I separate my support of Rangers from my political views.

David Taylor

In a way I suppose I am slightly influenced by people like Murray and Findlay. I am more likely to listen to the views of someone I respect rather than someone I don't.

Peter McFarlane

If the Conservatives are good enough for the top men at Ibrox then they're good enough for me.

Chris Rae

I vote Conservative. It's probably to do with the way I was brought up by my parents – those were the type of values they passed on to me. I'm also a friend of Donald Findlay so I would say that he has had an influence on me.

NEVERTHELESS, no matter how they arrive at their voting preferences, there are Rangers fans who do vote Conservative.

Brian Whitelaw

I consider myself a Conservative voter. I've never liked trade unions and I've always associated Labour with socialism/ communism/ trade unions.

Alistair Walker

I vote Conservative because they are more closely related to my ideals. I believe that the Conservative party strive to provide the individual with the opportunities to realise their ambitions, given all our differing abilities. This is not the same as saying the rich get richer and the poor get poorer. Sure, we are all born equal, but it's how we apply our talents and abilities during our lives that creates the gap.

Graham Donaldson

I would consider myself Conservative. My belief has always been that Labour will try and tax me more because I am successful and give that money to people who do nothing to deserve it. New Labour has moved from that position somewhat but only at national level. I don't think their values have penetrated to the local level where old communists still try to live off the back of those who have worked a little to get on.

David Taylor

I have always voted Tory. I tend to agree more with their policies regarding Northern Ireland and the maintenance of the Union.

Peter Ewart

I supported the Referendum Party in Glasgow in 1997. I would have supported the Conservatives, but the likelihood of them taking a Glasgow seat was less than zero. You could safely say I tend to the right.

Gordon Graham

I've always voted for the Conservatives. I believe they stand up for Britain better than the others. They stand up for the Ulster Unionists. I'm a Unionist. I believe very passionately in Great Britain, I don't like all the talk about Scotland going it alone. If it ever came to that, I think I would move to England. But in saying that the Tories are never going to do anything in Scotland. I liked Margaret Thatcher, I know a lot of people don't agree with that but she just kept her natural voters sweet. That's only natural in politics.

Alan Park

I would probably say I was a Conservative, certainly to the right. It's nothing to do with anything but the influence of my father. He was a managing director, middle class, so I suppose it was natural to vote Tory. I didn't vote at the last election as I feel one party is as bad as the other.

Jimmy Reid

I'm a Tory voter. It's the politics I've always believed in. My son is a Thatcherite and has stood as a Scottish Unionist councillor twice. If you look at the Labour party now I'm totally against it. They're spending more money talking about educating kids about homosexuality rather than helping the people of Scotland, so that doesn't encourage me to think about changing my vote to Labour.

THE PERCEPTION of Rangers fans as being sympathetic to right wing causes has, in part, been fuelled by their resemblance to the right wing extremists who follow the English national team and some other English club sides. These fans wreaked havoc during the 70s, 80s and 90s, wrapped in the Union flag and chanting the anti-IRA sentiments which are often heard wherever Rangers fans congregate. Organisations such as the National Front, primarily appealing to some Ibrox fans' sense of Britishness and notions of Loyalism, have attempted to court the Rangers support, appearing at games and attempting to sell literature and other wares. And like most modern day political organisations they alter their message to suit their audience. In England, right wing groups play upon people's race fears but in Scotland they focus on the anti-Irish and anti-Catholic element in the hope of some support.

Rangers fans have been associated with extremist activities in the past. After the Ibrox club played a European tie in Eindhoven in 1978 Nazi slogans were found daubed on walls which led journalist Brian Wilson to condemn the Ibrox fans. After the 1980 Old Firm 'riot final' at Hampden Park, James Gillespie, apportioning blame, claimed the National Front had linked up with Protestant organisations (and by implication Rangers fans) in Glasgow.[14] More recently, in September 1999 at a Rangers European tie in Holland (ironically in Eindhoven again), members of right wing group Combat 18 used the game as an excuse to travel for violence and although not all of the seventeen people arrested and convicted were Rangers fans, 'they travelled under the Rangers banner with Rangers fans amongst them'.[15]

This extreme right wing perception of Rangers fans led to attempts by some supporters to redress the balance. One fan complained, 'it disgusts me to see the racist scum at Ibrox' and urged Rangers fans to 'unite against fascism'.[16] In the mid 1990s some fans set up an organisation called 'Rangers supporters against the Nazis'.[17] However the organisation floundered and the chance to make some kind of positive gesture was lost. What are the current Ibrox fans feelings on this issue?

Stephen McLeod

The extremist groups who turn up at Ibrox are not widely supported by Rangers fans. What surprises me is that, although I rarely see them actually get a sale they are tolerated and what annoys me is that it gives the media manipulators another cheap shot at Rangers. We are tarred as Neanderthal skinhead racists.

Gordon Masterton

I think the groups like the BNP are just fascists and have no legitimate voice or concern with Rangers FC.

Scott Graham

I disagree with the views of many extremists such as the National Front, the British National Party and the Ku Klux Klan but I believe in the right to free speech. However, I do object to people thinking I support these causes because I attend Rangers games.

Peter Ewart

It's disgusting. It has absolutely no place outside Ibrox. It also does nothing to change the distorted image the Scottish media place upon our club. I remember an instance, a couple of season's back, just outside Ibrox Underground station, where a group of middle-aged men, long term season ticket holders, were having a real verbal go at two skinheads trying to sell Combat 18 filth. It looked like it might come to blows. The sooner these people get the message that they are definitely not wanted, the better.

David Taylor

I am dead against the likes of the BNP campaigning outside Ibrox. These people are racists and their literature is of no benefit to Rangers or Scotland.

Graham Donaldson

Unless there's a law against it who can stop it? The country is after all a democracy and we've fought hard for freedom of speech. It does only exist because of the weak immigration policies that Britain has held for many years. If people want that stuff let them have it. As long as they don't force their issues onto people, I've no objection.

David Nichol

It's only very occasionally you see the BNP or the NF at Ibrox and I've never seen anyone buy anything off them. But the thing is, if they had been stood outside Marks and Spencer would it have been the shop who was lambasted by the media? So why are Rangers held responsible? But Britain is a democracy and unless it's an illegal organisation or literature which contravenes the Public Order Act, then any group should be able to voice its opinions anywhere.

Peter McFarlane

Yes, you get these people hanging around sometimes at Rangers games and I think some of them would like to get the Rangers fans involved. Over the years at the Rangers games abroad I have sometimes seen a few dodgy characters, Chelsea fans I think, travelling with Rangers and hoping to get some trouble started. But Rangers fans are not into all that. These guys think all they have to do is shout 'Fuck the Pope' or 'UVF' and Rangers fans will come running, but it doesn't work like that.

THE CONSERVATIVE/Rangers empathy has a long and durable history. However, this link, especially amongst the supporters, is misleading in terms of gauging political sympathies at Ibrox.

Rangers fans have also had links with the Labour party, especially through the trade union movement which emerged and developed in the heavy industries in Scotland. Although there is no doubt the working class Tory model existed, many Rangers fans were trade union members and some undoubtedly held socialist convictions and attitudes associated with the traditional class war. Consequently, Rangers 'strongholds' like Bridgeton and Larkhall have consistently returned Labour MPs.[18]

Also, there is evidence that the, 'Orange vote', presumed to be strongly in favour of the Tory party, did in fact contradict these assumptions. Although the hierarchy of the Orange Order were overwhelmingly true blue Conservatives – some indeed, were MPs – the rank and file were not as sheepish in their attitudes. William Marshall notes that after World War II in a time of high unemployment and depression in many areas in Scotland, ordinary Orangemen, 'could see nothing intrinsically wrong with giving their support to a party (Labour) committed to policies of full employment social welfare and a free health service'.[19]

In Bradley's survey it was shown that 33% of Rangers fans were Labour voters.[20] The collapse of the Tory party in Scotland since the early 1990s, arguably pushes that figure even higher. Indeed, according to Walker, 'Given the current state of the Tory party in Scotland the vast majority of the Protestant working class (which obviously includes Rangers supporters) must be voting Labour and some, Scottish Nationalist'.[21]

John Frame

It's a tradition in my family to vote Labour and I'm heavily involved in the Trade Union movement, being a shop steward. At the start of the New Labour thing and their swing to the right I was totally against it. I was one of those people years ago, the least wee thing in the workplace, it was down tools and out on strike. It doesn't work anymore. People have got their cars and their houses and if you're continually on strike for the least wee thing, well, you've just got be sensible now. I have mellowed a bit in my politics and realise you have to work with management as opposed to being against them all the time.

Charlie McIntyre

I've always leaned towards the left although as a bluenose some would say I'm meant to be a Tory or whatever. My music taste is socialist in that I'm into punk groups and the Clash and groups like that, who are all basically left wing in their thoughts and I agree with that. Out of the politicians I've read about and listened to recently the guy who appeals to me most and talks the most sense is Tommy Sheridan of the Scottish Socialist Party. He has revived my interest in politics a little.

Gary Paul

I voted Labour the last time I voted. After the time of the Tories I thought they couldn't do any worse. I thought we could do with a change.

Bob Prescott

I have been a Labour enthusiast all my life, although at present it is a reluctant form of enthusiasm, as there simply isn't another party out there who I believe can deliver something more comprehensive. Being working class and living in a poor area soon tunes you into political parties who champion social causes.

Jim Black

I normally vote for Labour, although I never voted last time through disillusionment with them all. I am a socialist, probably because of my upbringing in Ayrshire. This area is a socialist area, back to the time of the mines. My father was a miner, my brother was a miner and so was my brother-in-law. I've also done my bit as a shop steward, where I work just now. But I'm also a unionist – there's no way I'd want the UK to break up. The problem with New Labour is that they are just glorified Tories. I wouldn't vote for the Scottish Socialist Party because it would mean breaking away from the union.

Dougie Brown

Being an ex-steelworker and trade union member it's not hard to see I was brought up to vote for Labour. I don't think I personally ever worked with anyone in Scotland who didn't vote Labour and there were plenty of bluenoses amongst them. It's the way it was in the 70s and 80s, trying to protect our jobs through the unions and watching the Tories close down the factories. I'll tell you, they were no friends of the Rangers fans, the Tories. I watched Thatcher decimate all the big industries in Scotland and do you know, we've never recovered yet. I see all these guys I used to work beside, Rangers and Celtic supporters, some have never worked since, or if they have it's as security guards and rubbish like that. Labour have to watch themselves though. They are getting as bad as the Tories in some cases. What happened to renationalising the railway and the electricity and things like that? They've went back on their word. Scottish Socialist Party may be the future but they're too small at the moment – it would be a wasted vote.

WHILST recognising that there are many Labour voters amongst Rangers supporters, there is an element in the make-up of the party in Scotland which provides some fans with the opportunity to complain of a sectarian bias against Protestants.

In Scotland, and in Glasgow in particular, there is a perception among some Rangers fans and others that a 'Catholic Mafia' has emerged and is thriving in the Labour party, especially in the City Chambers. This perception is fuelled by the facts that alongside a disproportionate amount of Catholic councillors serving in Glasgow, there hasn't been a Protestant Lord Provost for over twenty years. The 'mafia' claim is difficult to substantiate but one observer admitted that, 'in a council where the overwhelming majority are Catholic you do hear the phrase, 'he's one of us' with reference to religion'.[22]

Many Rangers fans suspected that Celtic were treated favourably by Glasgow City Council in dealing with their plans to redevelop Celtic Park. *The Glaswegian* newspaper reported that by 'sheer coincidence' the Labour administration realised that council houses in the shadow Celtic Park were in need of demolition just as refurbishment of the stadium got underway and the cleared land was then handed over to Celtic on a long lease.[23] Certainly the Labour party have always been keen to polish up their Celtic credentials. (One running joke in Glasgow is that Council meetings are held on matchdays in the Main Stand at Celtic Park.) A congratulatory parliamentary motion was put forward by a group of Scottish Labour MPs when Celtic won the League Championship in 1998 – the first motion of its kind since Celtic's previous title win in 1988.[24] This was grist to the mill of bluenoses who cried foul at the perceived favouritism by Labour towards Celtic.

However, it is not just in Glasgow that claims of Labour bias against Protestants have been made. The allegations of sectarianism and corruption which surfaced in local politics in 1994 against the Catholic-dominated Monklands Council, added fuel to the fire of those who advocated the Catholic conspiracy. The townspeople of Airdrie, predominantly Protestant, claimed they were discriminated against by Catholic Labour Councillors from neighbouring Coatbridge, in terms of resources and facilities as well as employment opportunities. Religious tensions awoke from their slumber and the by-election which followed the death of MP John Smith became a bitter and acrimonious battle.

The occasional political contributions which do appear in the fanzine *Number One* focus on the Catholic/Labour theme and are exemplified by the 'warning' to Rangers fans that the Labour candidate in the Hamilton by-election in 1999 was, 'another Tarrier for Tony (Blair)'. The same contributor, 'F.T.Pea' (*sic*) complained, somewhat mysteriously, that, 'the devious doctrine of multiculturalism' had been imposed on Britain, 'through the Labour party via the regional councils'.[25] Catholics were also criticised for using, 'their political organisation to gain enormous financial benefits for Catholic schools'.[26]

One contributor in *Follow Follow*, 'Cokey from Cumbernauld', claimed that Strathclyde Regional Council had wasted £500,000 of poll tax payers money helping Celtic and stated, 'I just thought the recent crop of socialists who have written in to *Follow Follow*, would like to know what their elected representatives are doing with our money'. [27] In a more nasty line of criticism, the Lord Provost of Glasgow, Alex Mosson was described as, 'republican filth (who) continues in the long line of provo armpits to besmirch the good name of the second city of the Empire'.[28]

The perceived Labour/Catholic theme has had good mileage in recent years amongst Rangers fans.

Dougie Brown

Come on, who are we trying to kid? I'm a Labour voter but I know the score as far as Glasgow is concerned. Pat Lally, Frank McAveety – they all run Glasgow to suit themselves and their own people. Even the Catholics I know admit as much and some are in the Labour party. They're all Celtic supporters in there, everybody knows it. . . . that's how Parkhead was done up without an objection on planning permission. Slipped through, nice and easy, your tickets will be waiting at the door boys!

Dave Nicol

I used to vote Labour but I wouldn't vote for them now because of the Scottish branch of the party, which I feel is sectarian and corrupt, in places like Monklands District Council and Glasgow District Council.

Robert McElroy

Catholic Mafia is perhaps the wrong phrase but how many Labour councillors in Glasgow are not Catholics? That can't be a good thing, if you consider they have to make decisions, for example on the closing of schools. Have these decisions been made purely on an economic basis? If you look at the situation with Celtic – the building of their stadium – that would never in a million years have been given planning permission had it not been who Celtic were and the fact that the councillors were overwhelmingly Catholic. Many of the committee were Celtic season ticket holders and that can't be right. I knew someone who was a local resident fighting the planning permission but he said he would as well have been banging his head off a brick wall.

Charlie McIntyre

I've heard Rangers fans, especially in Glasgow, saying Labour in Glasgow were always Celtic supporters.

Willie Torrie

I'm just totally against Labour. I think they're biased towards the Catholic faith. I think the Airdrie, Coatbridge thing tells its own story. You've got people like Ken Livingstone representing Labour. Well that also tells its own story.

Jimmy Reid

There's very much that idea of the Catholic involvement and you only have to look at Glasgow District Council for a start, I reckon 75-80% of it are of the Roman Catholic pers-uasion. I don't have anything against Catholics but it hasn't done Glasgow much good has it? I've always felt that over the years that I've voted Tory, there was always this slight Labour, pro-Church of Rome thing.

Colin Glass

You have the sectarian control of the Labour party, which I believe would dominate an independent Scotland. It is a fact that the majority of Glas-gow's Labour councillors are Catholics and a significant number are Celtic shareholders as well as fans. This is not a bigoted statement. It would be if it was false.

Jim Reid

I don't know if it is a myth. If you take facts the last seven Lord Provosts have been Catholics. I would hazard a guess that it would be more than coincidence that you could have seven without finding one Protestant within the party to redress the balance. They don't seem to be particularly bothered that this is common knowledge. I know some Protestants who are involved in Glasgow Labour politics and it is difficult for them to progress. When I've been in their company they've complained that they can't get anywhere.

RANGERS fans' claims that Labour have a Catholic bias, especially in Glasgow, perhaps rests as much on perception as fact. However, as the increasing reliance on spin doctors suggests, image in politics is important. A perception formed in Scotland throughout the 1980s and 90s was that of the Conservative party being run by English for the English. The Tories presided over the decimation of the traditional Scottish industries like coal and steel which led to massive unemployment figures in Scotland. In addition, the introduction of policies like the infamous poll tax and the personality of the Tory leader, Margaret Thatcher, led many Scots to feel that they were an anti-Scottish party, catering to the mainly Home Counties electorate on which their re-election depended.

Voters north of the border gradually realised that they were effectively powerless to shape or influence the make-up of the British government. From 1979, England consistently returned the Tories to power, despite the fact Scotland was voting Labour. What emerged to counter this powerlessness was a general growth in nationalism[29] and the strengthening of the Scottish National Party.

The Tory hegemony in Britain eventually ended due to a combination of poor leadership, internal party strife, and the successful modernisation of the 'New' Labour party who adopted the key Tory policies which catered for the self-same Home Counties electorate. When Labour came to power in the landslide election victory in May 1997 the Tories were wiped out in Scotland. The subsequent devolution referendum, promised by Labour in their election manifesto, recorded a 72% vote in favour of the bill and voting patterns made it clear that there was uniform support throughout Scotland.[30] It was a disaster for the Tories on two fronts. Not only did they manage to turn themselves into an unelectable shambles, they lost the argument against devolution which they had argued, was the first step on the road to the break-up of the Union.

The SNP, tapping into national discontent with Westminster politics, emerged a serious political player and showed they were capable of sustaining a strong and lasting challenge to the British constitutional *status quo*. Indeed, along with the implementation of the Scottish Parliament, the SNP has already changed the face of British politics. The party has encapsulated a modern feeling amongst many Scots, particularly the younger voters, that freedom and independence, which other states in Europe have had to address in the last twenty years, is an achievable and desirable goal. Some Rangers fans have taken to this idea.

Alison Dempster

I vote SNP. I always have done and at the moment I think I always will. I believe in independence and if it happens, I feel people outside the UK may begin to realise that we are a nation in our own right and that we have many things to be proud of.

Gordon Masterton

I'm all for independence. After all, can an independent Scotland be any worse than the current UK situation? I reckon it will happen within 20 years because the move to devolution will not be enough for some people.

Ian McColl

I've stood as a prospective SNP Councillor twice and I've been a member of the party for over thirty years. I'm a Scottish nationalist first and British second. I'm also a member of the Orange Order but in the SNP constitution it says that in a free and independent Scotland the Queen will remain head of state, much the same as she does in the commonwealth countries at the moment. So I'm still a royalist in that respect. You have to remember that the SNP in many ways is a one issue party and within it there are views from all across the political spectrum. They are all interested in a free and independent Scotland. SNP are now hitting Labour. At one time it was seen as a protest vote but attitudes have changed. The SNP are now the opposition in Scotland.

Kirsty Paterson

I voted for SNP in the last election. I would love to see a successful independent Scotland. However, there are areas such as defence where Scotland might struggle as an independent country, but I think it is something that will eventually come about.

Willie McLay

I'm a nationalist and have always voted so. Living in South Lanarkshire I've seen the results of blindly voting Labour or voting Conservatives because that's what Prods are supposed to do. Labour have long lost the ideals on which they were founded and the Tories aloofness and arrogance will never convince me they should decide what's in my best interests. I am an ardent Scot and don't feel comfortable with the Union although I don't think its demise is inevitable.

Des Ward

I do believe in the principle of an independent Scotland, although I do not believe that the Scottish National Party is mature enough to deliver it and certainly do not think that we are ready for it yet.

Allan Elder

A lot of fresh ideas are required to bring Scotland to the fore of European business, and I don't see that happening whilst we are still governed from London Every government that has run the country from London hasn't done anything for Scotland, especially the rural communities where extra taxation on fuel, heat etc have really hit hard. I think there will come a time when even the most staunch Unionist will say enough's enough.

Scott Graham

Since Britain is inevitably going to become part of a United States of Europe, I think Scotland would be better as an independent country within Europe. If Scotland were to stay out it would find it difficult to survive on her own. Independence is not inevitable but the more the Scottish Parliament is messed up, the higher the chances of independence are.

RANGERS fans who support other political parties have, unsurprisingly, different views on the issue of independence.

Robert McElroy

I shudder at the prospect of independence. . . the extremists in British politics belongs to the nationalists. The worst hostility I've experienced as a political activist was from the SNP and you can speak to the Labour activists and they will tell you the same thing. The last game Scotland played at Ibrox I was there and the pure hatred and bigotry – and God knows we should be used to bigotry attending matches in Glasgow – but the anti-English feeling from the Scotland fans was repulsive and revolting. The anti-English hostility in this country now is appalling.

Derek McLeod

Independence for Scotland is a joke, because if there was independence Scotland would just go straight in to Europe, Euro money and be totally ruled by Europe – not very independent.

Charlie McIntyre

I've always been a Unionist. I've nothing at all against England. I don't think

independence is inevitable, although it is obviously a possibility. The underprivileged in Scotland have a lot more in common with the underprivileged in England compared to the upper class in Scotland. If you have an independent Scotland then you'll end up with the North against the South, East against the West. I'm more concerned with the class issue in Britain. I'll always think of myself as working class and I've more in common, I feel, with a working class guy from Manchester or Liverpool than a Tory supporter in Scotland.

Brian Whitelaw

At a time when parts of the world are trying to come together, like the European Union, I can't see why Scotland would want to split from the United Kingdom and have another level of government.

Stuart Davidson

I believe independence for Scotland would be a big mistake as collectively, Scotland, England, Wales and Northern

Ireland will carry more clout within the EU. As I see it, Germany and France are the major players who will try and dictate policies, thus we don't want to weaken our position. We don't make a great job of negotiating now. Independence would only make things worse. Really, you have to look at the bigger picture rather than just look at the UK.

David Taylor

I am strongly against an independent Scotland. I feel in this day and age we should be breaking down barriers not building them.

Jim Black

Independence, I'm against it, definitely against it, I think we were getting on fine being ruled from Westminster without having to have a Parliament in Scotland to make Mickey Mouse decisions. For me, the Scottish Parliament is just a holiday camp for MPs. It's turned into a bit of a joke. I haven't heard of anything good to come out of it yet. You still get all these characters shouting we can go alone, we've got the resources, but the whisky industry is in decline, the oil fields are predominately owned

by America and Scandinavian countries, so I don't know where this idea of independence comes from.

Anthony Orr

Independence is a bad idea. Too much focus on being anti-English rather than pro-Scottish. SNP is very right wing and dangerous for Scotland. If they have their way you will need a passport to get across the border. Not the signal you want to be sending as Europe comes together. We need to stay in touch so that we have more of a say in what happens and to have any chance we need to do this as part of Britain.

John Frame

I'm against total independence. I work for a company called GEC, and big companies like that would soon leave Scotland, I firmly believe that, especially with the tax-raising the Nationalists are talking about.

Stephen Mcleod

I think we should stick to the status quo until a convincing proposal, as a positive for Scotland rather than a reaction, is put forward. I think this is the nationalist's biggest challenge and they have yet to develop such a proposal, or if they have they have failed to communicate it properly. Devolution is a nonsense, it's simply another layer of ineffective politicians to pay for and makes the operation of Westminster more difficult due to the West Lothian question.

Willie Torrie

I think we've stuck together 300 years and it's worked quite well. A lot of people are against the English but I'm certainly not. They've never done me any harm. We've been through two world wars, Argentina, you name it, and we've stuck together and it's been quite successful. I think there's too much We Hate the English. If we are going to be independent then it should be for the right reasons. A lot of people are still unsure. Devolution is half way – to me you're either independent or still British – to me it's just middle of the road and its going to cost us more in tax at the end of the day, so that's the bottom line. I think a lot of people are jumping on the Braveheart wagon and that's the wrong reason. I say to people who speak about it down here and say why? We're quite well-off compared to other parts of the world.

A FEATURE of British society in recent decades has been a questioning of the role of the monarchy. There is an increasing groundswell of opinion which argues that, in a modern democratic country, the institution is something of an anachronism. And the threat to its existence, especially in its present mode, cannot be lightly dismissed. In the drive towards a more meritocratic society, another archaic British institution, the House of Lords, has recently been 'modernised' and its long term future is in doubt.

Some of Britain's Commonwealth countries are also addressing the constitutional issue. The role of the monarchy was debated in Australia, and in a referendum in November 1999, the Australian people voted narrowly to keep the Queen as the head of state. However, the issue was far from settled.

Traditionally, many Rangers fans, often focusing on the Protestant/British aspect of the monarchy, were among the most fervent Royal Family supporters in Scotland. The Queen, in particular, was held in high regard at Ibrox and a characteristic of Rangers matches for decades was the singing of the national anthem (although this has declined in frequency in the past decade or so). So how do modern-day Rangers fans feel about the monarchy?

Alan Park

I would say I was all for it. It gives Britain a good name throughout the world. People can see Britain as a stable and good country. Certainly the Queen and the Queen Mother are respected although some of the younger ones like Charles and Andrew seem to be making a mess of things and they certainly won't get respect.

Ian McColl

I think the monarchy will change to more like the Scandinavian countries and the Netherlands where they are a figurehead and that is basically it. I don't think they're on the way out. I think you have to have a figurehead like that. I'm a little disillusioned with some of the hangers-on down the Royal list but I'm all in favour of the top brass.

Stephen Macleod

The monarchy is a vital symbol of our British identity, respected and envied by the rest of the world. In capitalist terms, they are also huge money earners in terms of tourism.

Jim Reid

Yes, I am in favour of the monarchy. But we should be careful. Recently a Scottish MSP introduced a motion to introduce a situation where the monarch can marry a Catholic. I'm a born again Christian, and the Bible is very close to my heart. I feel that it is quite important that the defender of the faith, the monarch, is part of the faith. It would be very wrong if the monarch wasn't of the faith. If he wasn't then you would be as well having a president like America.

Ian McHutchison

The monarchy is a good thing and I think it will remain in the UK for the foreseeable future. It gives us a sense of identity and assists in foreign relations. From a purely economic viewpoint it plays a vital part in procuring inward investment. I have a great deal of respect for Charles but I don't think he will ever have the same emotive effect on the Rangers fans as the Queen who is a tremendously strong and dignified woman. Having said that, as the awe in which the monarchy is held shrinks, so does the deference paid to the monarch. You will find it's a lot of the older Rangers fans who have a deep-seated love and respect for the institution and the younger ones are just standing and singing because that is what is expected of them.

Willie Torrie

I'm a believer in the monarchy but I think it could do with a wee shake. I think they should be pulled into the year 2000. I'm a bit worried about the talk of involving Catholics in it because it would be going back on an old rule and I think that the Protestant aspect is an important part.

Chris Rae

I'm one hundred per cent behind the monarchy. I think it's an important part of being British and I consider myself British. I hold a British passport not a Scottish one.

Jimmy Reid

I'm for the monarchy as the head of the country, because what's the alternative? A Fidel Castro or a Bill Clinton? I wouldn't like to lose it. Outside anything else I think the likes of the Yanks, they all love to come over and see it, the pomp and circumstance that goes with it.

Gary Paul

I still support them. They still do a good job although they've had some bad publicity over the past couple of years. The Queen especially does a good job promoting the country throughout the world.

OTHER fans are less positive about the future of the monarchy.

Alistair Walker

I don't give much thought to the monarchy. They are, after all, only PRs for the country. In fact, I sense less respect for the monarchy generally. Perhaps the allegiance to the monarchy at Rangers was borne out of anti-Irishness and anti-Catholicism more than a true allegiance to the concept.

William McLay

I'm not a monarchist. I did serve in the armed forces and I was raised in Larkhall and I have gone to Ibrox since I was eight, but I am still not and never have been a monarchist. An independent Scotland would be the ideal situation to rid the people of this archaic establishment. And you would have to ask if they would want anything to do with us anyway. Going on previous experience we are of little value to them, no more than a big shooting estate.

Anthony Orr

Not a great fan of the monarchy . . . thankfully they seem to becoming less and less significant.

Allan Elder

I don't respect the Queen or Charles. I have no time for any of the Royals. If we must have a figurehead, I'd rather see someone elected. . . when independence arrives, I think the Royals will be out of Scotland.

Dougie Brown

The monarchy is not something I think about too much to be honest. I'm not one of these God Save the Queen people, no way. Prince Philip, I mean, has that guy got a friend in the whole world? And Charles, he's going around talking to plants. I mean, how can they kid on they represent me, the working man in Scotland? I'll tell you something, Rangers fans are only believers because of the Protestant thing. If they had to turn to Catholicism tomorrow then the Rangers fans would be in an uproar and they'd soon turn against them.

Kirsty Paterson

To be honest I couldn't care less about the monarchy.

FROM WHAT empirical sources and anecdotal evidence we can muster, there does seem to be a diverse range of political views and interests amongst the Ibrox faithful. Some attitudes clearly reflect a different political era, a time of more definite ideological difference between left and right, whereas others recognise the changing face of British and Scottish politics. There are few radically different policy variations between the main political parties (except, obviously, the SNP) which makes it increasingly difficult for voters to differentiate between them.

However, given the history of the Ibrox club there will be those who will be shocked to find that what were traditional political bedrock beliefs of Rangers fans – the monarchy and the Union – no longer command unquestioning support. Both institutions are coming under increasing pressure from various sections of British society and some Rangers supporters subscribe to the prospect of modernisation if not total abolition. In many ways the varied and complex political views of the scattered Ibrox support is a microcosm of Scottish society. It seems acceptable among Rangers fans to be Unionist and to the left just as it is okay to be nationalist and in favour of the monarchy. These are legitimate political views and are prevalent throughout Scotland.

But despite there only being a minority of fans who consider themselves Conservative/right wing, Rangers FC and their followers will continue to find it difficult to shake off that image. Some Rangers supporters retain somewhat traditional political allegiances to a by-gone age of Union, Empire, Queen and country. In Scotland as a whole, these political views are unquestionably declining. Some Rangers fans, especially those who inhabit the world of Rangers fanzines, do their best to reinforce the notion that Ibrox is a little piece of Scotland that will be forever British. The Conservative image of the Ibrox club fostered by some of its staff and officials also has an impact on how people see the Ibrox fans. There can be no question that board members of all football clubs have always been, almost by definition, rich businessmen or professionals. Thus, as Bill Murray notes, it can hardly be surprising that traditional Conservative values were likely to prevail amongst these type of people.[31] There are other factors, such as songs and flags, which reinforce the right wing perception if not truly reflecting reality. The Rangers section of Hampden Park in the 1999 Scottish Cup final was akin to the 'last night of the Proms' such was the plethora of Union flags and the lusty renditions of 'Rule Britannia'. And although these symbols belongs to no particular political party, they have been hi-jacked over the years not only by the Conservatives but also by the extreme far right groups thus becoming increasingly despised in the wider Scottish society. A by-product of the right wing perception of the fans and the club has been the attempted infiltration by right wing extremists who feel an affinity with all things Rangers. Although they are evidently not well received, the fact that they feel comfortable and are tolerated at Ibrox is a poor reflection on all those who have Ibrox allegiances.

However, notions of left wing, anti-Royal and/or pro-independence Rangers fans is fine in theory but discussion would still best be kept away from Ibrox. A football environment is not normally conducive to reasoned political debate and thus fans with less conventional 'Rangers style' political views, do well to keep silent. It would be a brave, if foolish man who stood outside Ibrox preaching the virtues of communism or socialism. Even recruiting for mainstream political parties like Labour and the SNP could prove a dangerous pastime.

For many Rangers supporters the issue of religion, although not necessarily making them vote positively for any one party, does put some off voting for Labour. The feeling among some Rangers fans that the Labour Party in Scotland has developed into a biased Catholic organisation may linger for years to come, although it must be said than an investigation into the 'Monklands affair' found no concrete evidence of sectarianism. The Labour party has long been a vehicle, some would say the only one, for the Catholic community to improve their standing in Scottish society. They can hardly be blamed for grasping that opportunity. For most Protestants who don't support Rangers, the issue has been give little credence. There is still huge support for Labour in Glasgow and indeed all over the country.[32]

Nationalists, absurdly seen by some 'loyal' fans as traitors, would also be ill-advised to voice their opposition to the United Kingdom wherever Rangers fans congregate. The republican aspect of Nationalism, although the SNP claim the Queen would remain a figurehead in an independent Scotland, would be sure to inspire animosity amongst Rangers fans, some of whom froth at the mouth at the sight of a St Andrews flag or the sound of 'Flower of Scotland' (issues which will be discussed in more detail later).

Despite what conclusions one might deduce from this chapter on the political allegiances of Rangers fans, there are several factors which need recognition. Politics amongst the Scottish population as a whole is a subject which inspires apathy, evident in the poor 58% turn-out for the first Scottish Parliament elections.[33] Politics and politicians are held in low esteem and in this respect at least, research of Rangers fans on this subject showed them to differ little from the rest of the population. Of all the issues raised in this book, politics was the one which inspired the least enthusiasm among respondents.

Although a Scottish Parliament has heralded a new dawn in British politics, the early results are not encouraging. Holyrood has done little to allay the fears many felt that a halfway house between the *status quo* and independence would not work. Already there have been tensions between Westminster and Holyrood on issues such as 'Section 28' and student funding which have served to highlight political differences between Scotland and England. In addition, the seemingly endless early debates over MSPs' wages, holiday entitlements and indeed the actual building of the new Parliament has overshadowed much of the political proceedings. The new Scottish Parliament is arguably Westminster writ small and so far political participation north of the border seems unlikely to increase.

One interesting footnote when discussing the political allegiances of Rangers fans is that on evidence available and anecdotal information volunteered for this book, they are less 'unionist' in their outlook than Celtic supporters. Celtic fans in the Bradley survey displayed an overwhelming propensity to vote Labour who, by any terms of reference, are strongly in favour of the idea of the United Kingdom. Only 4% of Celtic fans were SNP voters in comparison to 14% of Rangers fans.[34] Should the Ibrox fans therefore, hand over their Union flags to their more 'loyal' counterparts across the city?

4

Rangers fans and Scotland

WHEN RANGERS' Danish star Brian Laudrup was loudly booed by a section of the Scotland support in a friendly international between Scotland and Denmark in March 1998, ironically at Ibrox, it wasn't the usual abuse that home fans reserve for the most talented opposition player. It was because Laudrup was a Rangers player. The fans' reaction was a clear demonstration of the change in the make-up of the Scotland support and of the anti-Rangers culture that exists.[1]

For the Rangers fans who were in the crowd or who watched later on television, it was the last straw. Many phoned and wrote to newspapers condemning the treatment of the player.[2] Some vowed never to support the national team again. Throughout the century, up until around the 1980s it would have been unlikely that a Rangers player, of whichever side, would be jeered so viciously by the Scotland support – primarily because the Ibrox fans made up the bulk of it. But the composition of the Scotland following has changed dramatically over the past twenty years and is peculiar in the sense that the majority are not Old Firm fans but followers of teams such as Aberdeen, Motherwell, Dundee and Kilmarnock. Former

Rangers player Ian Ferguson noted how his poor treatment at the hands of Scotland fans was partly a result of his Ibrox connection.[3] All a far cry from the time when Scotland matches were a second home for most bluenoses.

Politically and culturally, for much of the twentieth century there were no dilemmas for Rangers supporters in terms of their attitudes towards the national team. The Scottish/Protestant identity of Rangers Football Club, along with strong Ibrox representation in the Scotland teams, made supporting the national team a natural extension for Rangers fans. They rejoiced in the knowledge that the Ibrox club had become, 'Scottish sport's premier institution, acquiring international recognition and featuring in such matches of immense public interest as the clash with Moscow Dynamo in 1945'.[4] Scottish nationalism was still struggling to gain momentum and Ibrox fans, like most Scots, were comfortable with their dual Scottish/British nationality which still allowed a measure of cross border rivalry.

Rangers players were synonymous with the national team and generations of Ibrox fans were brought up on the glorious Scotland victories which owed much to Ibrox. The Scotland national team's most famous triumphs had been against England and such Ibrox greats as Alan Morton, George Young, Jim Baxter and John Greig enhanced their reputations in the dark blue of Scotland. Morton is revered for being part of the great Wembley Wizards side which beat England 5-1 in 1928. Young and Greig were outstanding captains of both Rangers and Scotland. And Baxter is generally accepted as Scotland's greatest ever player and his performances against England at Wembley in 1963 and 1967 still talked about in reverential tones.

The structure of international football also played a part in the Rangers/Scotland relationship. Up until the early 70s Scotland had yet to make their mark in terms of qualifying on a regular basis for World Cups and European Championships. It was the Home International games against Northern Ireland, Wales and especially England, which were important dates on the football calendar. A great Scottish footballing culture of the 'Wembley Weekend' developed through the years, with thousands of Scots descending on London for the bi-annual game on trips often organised through offices, workshops, factories, Masonic halls, social clubs and supporters clubs.

Rangers had the biggest support in Scotland with Ibrox sympathies extending from most clubs in Scotland in a way which no longer exists. And Scotland played their home games in Glasgow where, for most of the century, the bulk of the Rangers support lived. Thus, attendances at Scotland matches, both home and away, were boosted to a large extent by bluenoses.

Robert McElroy

I watched Scotland play every game at Hampden between 1965 and 1983 except for the time they played Wales in 1972 when I was in Barcelona for Rangers' Cup Winners Cup final. There is no question that up until at least the early 70s that the majority of the Scottish crowd was Rangers supporters, sometimes as much as seventy per cent. The Scotland managers in that period, the full-time ones like Brown and McColl, were ex-Rangers players so that strengthened the link. You have to remember that in the 60s they played 'God Save the Queen' before the match and it was sung then the same way it is sung nowadays by England fans at Wembley. There was a minority of those who booed it of course, but they were the Celtic fans.

Stuart Daniels

I was a Scotland supporter, of course I was. In fact the majority of Scotland fans were Rangers fans. . . for every five Rangers fans there was about one Celtic fan. I went to all the Scotland games at Wembley, 1959, 1961 the 3-2 game in '67. My father took me. That's the way it was then.

Tam Plunkett

I was always a Scotland supporter when I was younger and lived in Scotland. In the 60s it was mostly Rangers fans who followed them, and sometimes you could hear 'The Sash' being belted out by large sections of the crowd.

John Allardyce

I remember going to Scotland games at Hampden and it was all Rangers fans in the Rangers end. . . you never got Scotland fans singing 'Walk on'. I first went to Wembley in 1975 when I was in first year at secondary school. There was about six buses outside the Luton Rangers supporters club to take us all to Wembley. I think only one bus left from the Celtic club. They say Celtic players were booed. I suppose some were but in the case of McClair most of the Rangers fans had stopped supporting Scotland by then. McClair was rubbish, that's why he was booed.

Dougie Brown

I was brought up close to Hampden so I went to all the Scotland games there. I remember the Hampden games in the 70s. Rangers and Celtic fans used to segregate themselves although there were much more Rangers fans than Celtic fans. I didn't care what end I got in but you could always hear the extra cheers for the Celtic players in the Celtic end and vice versa. The cover in the Rangers end made it seem louder though and it wasn't unusual to see Rangers scarves up on the terrace. Celtic fans used to complain that their players were booed by Rangers fans but that isn't true. Well, maybe on the odd occasion when for instance Jimmy Johnstone was playing ahead of Henderson. I used to go to all the Wembley weekends, my first one was in 1979 when I was seventeen, 3-1 we got beat. When you're there it's just a brilliant weekend and although you want Scotland to win it's not a big deal if they get beat. I mean it's not as if you had to face an Englishman at work on the Monday, is it? There was some guy with a big lambeg drum one year and a few guys had their flutes and all of a sudden we've got a band marching round Trafalgar Square and up to Leicester Square. Rangers fans were coming out from all the pubs, it was magic, all singing and dancing. The Scotland game was forgotten about. But at that time the Scotland team was made up of Rangers and Celtic players and the Anglos. That's why the Hampden crowds were so big, it was Old Firm fans. Nowadays, it's all different, you have to give free tickets to schoolkids to get a crowd.

Brian Donaghy

I went to Wembley for the first time to see Scotland in 1973, when I was nine. My grandfather took me. At that time and in the following years there was a lot of Rangers fans going, I would say about fifty per cent. Now I would say it was ten per cent. Rangers supporters clubs used to run buses, Paisley Central, Paisley North End, they had buses going. Mind you, they weren't all Rangers fans on the buses but the majority were.

Charlie McIntyre

I used to go to the Scotland games when I was younger. My dad sometimes took me and we would go to the stand but if I went with my mates I always made sure I went into the Rangers end. I wouldn't go to the Celtic end. I remember Derek Johnstone and Peter McCloy playing against Brazil

in 1973. I was also down at Cardiff the time Stein died. At that time only Davie Cooper was a regular and he used to get a special cheer from the Rangers end. I used to go with the jersey on with Cooper on the back. I even got a Bonnie Scotland tattoo when I was 18.

Colin Glass

Yes, I used to go to the home matches and the ones at Wembley. I was also at the 1974 World Cup in Germany. I would say roughly sixty per cent of Scotland fans were Rangers fans in those days. Apart from the Scotland versus England game which was always sold out, the busiest part of the ground was always the Rangers end, and the Scotland fans used to sing 'We'll support you ever more' and 'God Save the Queen' which were Rangers type songs. But the fans never sang 'Walk-on' although every other set of fans sang it at league games. Occasionally someone would try and start it and they would get drowned out by a loud chorus of boos. The selection of Jimmy Johnstone instead of an on-form Willie Henderson provoked a bad reaction from the 'Scotland' fans at one or two games and the number of times that the names of Colin Stein, Sandy Jardine, Willie Henderson were chanted clearly showed a great affection for those particular players. When I travelled to the 1974 World Cup there was only one Gers player in the Scottish squad, as that season had been a disaster for Rangers. I was on a plane with fans from all over Scotland and even then, Rangers had the most fans, in our party anyway. Fans from all the clubs were there though and we got on well.

Alan Russell

My dad took me to my first Scotland game in 1969 or 1970. It was against England at Hampden and Colin Stein should have got a penalty. There was a minibus went through and most of us were Rangers fans. On the way home after the game the men were all drunk and they started to sing party songs. I was a bit confused but I loved it. When I got older I used to go to all the Scotland games at Hampden and went to a few in Wales, Wembley and even Windsor Park. At that time there was always lots of Rangers fans, especially at Windsor Park. One year there was even a flute band on the boat going to the game and nobody minded. It wouldn't happen now.

Garry Lynch

I used to go to Scotland games as did most Rangers supporters. It was a good atmosphere at games because there wasn't the same tension as watching Rangers. There was self-segregation at the games so the Rangers end was packed and the Celtic end could be three-quarters empty. They used to play 'God Save the Queen' before the games and I would be singing it and people would be giving me hassle. Often it was the same people who would be singing it on a Saturday who were booing it on a Wednesday.

SEVERAL factors can explain the alienation of a large section of the Rangers support from the national team. One aspect, perhaps unsurprisingly given the man's impact at Ibrox, dates back to the time of Graeme Souness. When Souness arrived at Rangers he immediately laid the foundations for Rangers' subsequent dominance in Scotland with a string of expensive

English signings and woke the Ibrox club from a slumber to win the league at the first time of asking.

However, Souness's attitude and methods were not to everyone's liking. His thinly disguised contempt for the quality within Scottish football manifested itself in the importing of top class English players. This strategy didn't go down too well outside Ibrox. At a time when the English-dominated Conservative party were becoming deeply unpopular in Scotland, an increasingly successful Rangers became a focal point for anti-English sentiment from supporters of other teams. The seeds of an anti-Rangers culture were sown. This phenomenon will be discussed later but first we should look at the antagonistic relationship that developed between the SFA and Rangers.

Souness's disciplinary problems brought Rangers into endless conflict with the SFA. The tone was set right from his first league game for Rangers as player/manager against Hibs at Easter Road in season 1986/87. Souness was sent off and eight others were booked and such was the outcry after the game that the SFA gave Souness an extra three match ban on top of an automatic one match. Souness was again dismissed later in that season against Aberdeen on the day Rangers won the league title and early in the next season he was again sent off against Celtic which effectively ended his career as a player at Ibrox. As a manager his troubles with the ruling bodies continued and he received fines and touchline bans, one of which he ignored, and this got him into further trouble. Souness's whole time at Ibrox was set against a backdrop of constant battles with the SFA.[5]

When Souness left Ibrox in 1991 to join Liverpool many supporters claimed he had been hounded out by the SFA. Souness himself did little to contradict that notion enigmatically claiming he had 'taken the club as far as he had been allowed'.[6]

Such was the feeling of hostility that *The Rangers Historian* called for Rangers fans, 'to boycott all international matches under the auspices of the SFA, in order to teach these people that they cannot treat Britain's greatest football club like dirt'.[7] The same publication also, 'saluted the decisions of both Andy Goram and Duncan Feguson to turn their backs on the Scottish national side'.[8] Thus, one of the legacies of the Souness era was a hostile relationship with Scottish football's ruling bodies which has continued to the present day.

Ian Campbell

When I was younger I was split 50-50 between Rangers and Scotland but that's no longer the case now, no way. For me it goes back to the time of Souness and his first few years at Ibrox when he was continually at war with the SFA and the Scottish League. This put the Rangers fans' backs up and this has developed over the years to the extent that Rangers fans feel the SFA has got it in for them. Most of the supporters who travel on my bus feel the same way.

Follow Follow (96)

'It is hard enough to feel too much sympathy for Ally McCoist MBE. In my opinion he gave up being a Ranger years ago. His career was curtailed because he wanted to play for a shower of anti-Rangers scum. I don't want players playing for an anti-Rangers organisation.'

Stuart Daniels

The lack of interest amongst the Rangers fans in the national team goes back to the 80s when, the SFA started to shaft Rangers and they haven't stopped since. Remember Duncan Ferguson got a 12-match ban and there just the other day, Stephan Mahe gets off!

Craig Knox

As for the SFA I've not liked them since the days of Souness . . . they were always looking to fine us for something.

Robert McElroy

Rangers fans drifted away from Scotland for many reasons. Over a long period of time it has been perceived, rightly or wrongly, that the SFA have been anti-Rangers. In fact it goes back to 1969 when Colin Stein got sent off in March and his suspension coincided with the Scottish Cup final in May. It was almost to the day and he missed the final against Celtic. Duncan Ferguson is another good example. Rangers had problems with Jim Farry, he was a disaster.

Ally Williamson

A few years ago I began to be turned off supporting the Scotland team. Now I have no time for them at all. To be honest I'd rather see Northern Ireland or England do well, rather than Scotland. This may be a sad attitude to have but it's real nonetheless and I know many Rangers fans who feel the same way. . . we have been hung out to dry by the SFA in the last decade, they are definitely anti-Rangers. It's one rule for Rangers and one for the rest. Take Ian Ferguson, he got a six match ban for spitting at an opponent, while Mark Viduka received no extra

punishment for the same thing. Incredible. Henrik Larsson and Alan Stubbs both dished out abusive signs to opposition supporters, yet nothing gets done . . . Souness, Gazza and big Duncan Ferguson have been hounded out by these freeloaders. I'm not looking for special treatment just equal treatment.

Colin Glass

I'll tell you why Rangers fans don't follow Scotland anymore, because the blatant anti-Rangers bias delivered from Park Gardens at every opportunity.

Tam Plunkett

I think a lot of fans think the way I do about the way we are treated by the SFA. I remember a few years ago when Rangers had, I believe, twenty eight players down with the flu and they asked for a postponement of a league game against Hibs. It was a reasonable request given the circumstances but they were refused.

HOWEVER, if Rangers fans feel the SFA have done them no favours, then the national team selections have also met with disapproval from within the Ibrox stands.

Andrew Nesbitt

There has been a lot of annoyance at Craig Brown over the amount of Celtic players he has picked in recent years. We feel players like Ian Ferguson who did't always make the first team at Ibrox were still good enough for Scotland. Brown's policies annoy in other ways. I mean picking guys like Matt Elliot and Neil Sullivan, no heart, these guys, you'd be better off picking Rab Douglas from Dundee.

Number One (87)

'His (Craig Brown) public feuding with and non-selection of Rangers players while at the same time flooding the squad with inferior Celtic players has turned off the bulk of what was the 'natural' Scottish support.'

Dougie Brown

The way Craig Brown cut his nose off to spite his face with Richard Gough was a disgrace. Gough was easily the best centre half Scotland had but Brown continually left him out, because he had slagged Roxburgh. Childish, that's all it was. And they're trying to make Brown out to be a Rangers supporter!

Ally Williamson

There has been the managers of Scotland especially Craig Brown. He has consistently picked lesser Celtic players over superior Rangers ones. I give you McKinley, Boyd, Burley over Gough, Robertson, McCall and Ian Ferguson. It's funny how Brown's fall-outs are always with Rangers players.

HAVING looked at the part Graeme Souness, the SFA and Scotland managers have played in the decline in Ibrox support for the national team, we can turn to the complex and often confusing questions of the Ibrox identity. Rangers have become, in terms of players, increasingly less of a Scottish club. Since the mid 1980s the signing policies of Graeme Souness and subsequently Walter Smith were geared towards European success and this resulted in an increasing propensity towards non-Scots. Dick Advocaat has now taken this policy on to another level and there are now few Scottish first team regulars. Thus the Scottish identity of the club has grown weaker.

This development has coincided with an era of growing nationalism and Nationalism in Scotland and Rangers fans' traditional dual Scottish/ British nationality is no longer shared by the majority of the football fans in Scotland. The presence of Englishmen at Ibrox, especially high profile players like Terry Butcher and Paul Gascoigne, gave the xenophobic and racist elements amongst Scottish football fans an easy target. At away grounds these players were jeered for their nationality as much as their blue jerseys. Thus, over the years the Ibrox fans have become marginalised and they are castigated by other supporters for their perceived identity crisis. To emphasise their 'Scottishness' opposition fans (Celtic's apart) taunt Rangers supporters by singing 'Flower of Scotland' and waving St Andrew's flags. Rangers fans react by showing Union flags, and singing 'Rule Britannia'. In recent times this identity issue has escalated and although you can find many English, Dutch and Northern Ireland flags and replica tops among the Ibrox crowd, similar Scottish symbols are harder to find.

However, it would be wrong to assume that these seemingly anti- Scottish attitudes at Ibrox meet approval from all the fans. Whilst some supporters are happy to be considered 'British' others retain their keen sense of Scottish identity and resent the implication that they are not Scottish. The issue has split the Gers support.

Graham Gardner

I first saw Scotland in 1973, got the flag and all that and I have been interested in them ever since. I used to go to the Home Internationals and I eventually joined the Scotland Travel Club. At the Scotland games when I go, there isn't a lot talked about Rangers and Celtic although there are Rangers fans in the small crowd I go with. There's a big ex-pats group from Corby who go and there are a few Rangers fans amongst them. It really annoys me when I hear all that nonsense with the 'Flower of Scotland'. I feel it's my national anthem, not 'God Save the Queen'. Rangers are a Scottish club and should retain their national identity.

Ian Campbell

The jeering of the 'Flower of Scotland' makes me feel uncomfortable as I think Rangers fans should promote the notion of Rangers being Scotland's number one team. When in Europe I feel they are representing Scotland more than Britain. It disappoints me

that I rarely see the St Andrew's flag at the Rangers games and it's stupid to see Scottish Rangers fans with England strips on. Celtic fans get slagged for wearing Republic of Ireland shirts but Rangers fans are just as bad wearing England shirts.

Tony Orr

Rangers fans booing the 'Flower of Scotland' – to be honest, I feel ashamed. Although we are all part of Britain nothing stirs the blood more than the 'Flower of Scotland'. If you've ever been to Murrayfield it certainly gives the players and the fans a lift. . . although saying that there aren't many Scottish players in the Rangers or Celtic first team anymore. At the games Rangers fans should also only have St Andrew's flags. Living and watching football in London now the Union flag is usually only flown by teams with strong racist links. It no longer really represents British people. In Glasgow it takes on a whole new meaning that is nothing to do with football.

Dougie Brown

Sometimes I sit there and cringe when I hear the fans jeering the 'Flower of Scotland'. It just makes us look stupid and the opposition fans know it winds us up. Well some of us anyway. Nobody in the main stand where I sit jeers, it's mainly those supporters nearer the away fans. I'd rather we had the Scotland flags on show but at least there's not so many Ulster flags nowadays.

Craig Knox

I think at Ibrox the supporters should have St Andrew's flags and Union Jacks. I mean, Rangers have British-based support. . . I think the young ones take the Union Jacks because they are the club colours, but they're not sure what it means.

Stuart Daniels

The introduction of high profile Englishmen like Terry Butcher and Chris Woods in the Souness era added to an existing British identity and at that time Rangers fans liked to see England do well. In fact on our bus there are more England supporters than Scotland supporters.

Derek McAvoy

All Scottish clubs and their fans hate Rangers, so why should Rangers fans sit beside them at Scotland games.

Robert McElroy

The growth of nationalism in Scotland has put some Rangers fans off. That's why I stopped going to Scotland games in 1983. It was during a General Election and I was doing some canvassing for the Conservative party and went straight to the game. It was a Home International. There was so much anti-English songs, and anti-English hatred, it was not compatible with what I was about. It's got worse since then. Even the Scottish press commented upon the anti-English sentiment, pure racism in actual fact, which was displayed last October at Tynecastle when Scotland played Estonia.[8] The Tartan Army are not the happy-go-lucky guys they like to think they are with their ludicrous 'See you Jimmy' hats. They are racists.

Drew Failes

As far as the flags which Rangers fans bring to the ground go, St Andrew's flags are okay but since we are still part of the

UK I don't see why they shouldn't bring the Union flag if they feel like it. I'm not sure about the Red Hand of Ulster, since it is after all about a football match and not reliving the Battle of the Boyne.

Colin Glass

The Tartan Army? Their treatment of Brian Laudrup was shameful and I would not wish to be associated with such small-minded individuals.

Tam Plunkett

The St Andrew's flag is considered equal in status and either one can be flown and is proper. I would like to see both flags flown by our support. We are a Scottish team after all but 'Flower of Scotland' is not our national anthem. It is amazing that when Scottish supporters sing about a battle with the English in 1314, that is not considered sectarian, yet when we sing a few songs about a battle fought only 300 years ago, then that is sectarian. I deplore the racism directed against the English people in Scotland and I gladly sing 'Rule Britannia', happy in the fact that we as Scots were part of that glorious era. I do however, also deplore the raising of the arm in that disgusting salute, whilst singing.

Derek Macleod

Rangers fans should bring only Union Jacks, Red Hand of Ulster flags and England flags to the games at Ibrox and the away games. There should never be any Scotland flags. I have seen them before and I can't stand it. We are a British team, not Scottish. The Scottish flags are flown by the people who are pro-Scottish independence and anti-British and anti-Monarch. The red hand of Ulster and England flags are definitely welcome because Ulster is a Protestant country and pro-Britain as is England. It is the Tartan Army, independence and Catholics in Scotland who hate Britain, but Rangers are a British club and always will be.

Colin Glass

We are both Scottish and British. Rangers fans should feel comfortable about bringing the flag of whichever country they come from. My personal favourite is the Union flag. No wonder Rangers fans boo the 'Flower of Scotland'. It is an overtly racist dirge. It contains more anti-English sentiment than 'The Sash' does anti-Catholic sentiment, yet apparently this is to be frowned upon. Rags like the *Daily Record* preach double standards like this all the time.

Ally Williamson

Rangers fans have always stood by the Union flag because it demonstrates the links between Rangers, Scottish and Ulster society. It also shows we are proud to be British but that doesn't mean we don't like Scotland the country. St Andrew's cross is an important part of the flag. It is a flag which represents the different back-grounds, yet the common identity of the Rangers support. St Andrew's flags have become less popular because Scottish-ness is now equated with nationalism. The Red Hand of Ulster flag will always be welcomed by Rangers fans as it represents a large part of our community and demonstrates the distinct Protestant identity of Northern Ireland. It's funny how those who are so vociferous in condemning Protestant/loyalist anthems and celebrat-ions of the Battle of the Boyne are often the same people who glorify Bannockburn. The hypocrisy and arrogance of such

people is seen through by many of the Rangers fans. But there been a sea change in Scottish society in the last twenty years. Scottishness has been hijacked, in my opinion, by nationalists and separatists. As a Unionist, I can't swallow supporting Scotland with the kind of people who follow them. Rangers have always attracted supporters from across the UK. Most of us from Scotland are Protestant and Unionist. When you add those from Northern Ireland and England, it's no wonder we sing songs like 'Rule Britannia'. Our songs reflect our identity, and it's an identity that has become increasingly isolated from what Scottishness means today.

Derek McAvoy

Scottish flags and Union flags should be encouraged at Ibrox. We have many fans in Northern Ireland, so their flag should also be welcomed.

RANGERS fans have turned away from Scotland for several reasons which include a dislike of the SFA and team politics, notions of nationality and an antagonistic relationship with fans of other teams in Scotland. However, there are more straightforward and conventional reasons why Ibrox fans (as well as other football supporters) are loathe to attend Scotland matches.

Mike Watt

I went to a few Scotland games in the 60s when Colin Stein played, a few matches against England, but now I find the national team boring and predictable. . . with very little style. When I watch them on the television I find myself going off to make tea during the match.

Frank Geddes

I've been to a few games when I was younger, and you have to remember in those days it took up to seven hours to go to Glasgow, but I wouldn't dream of going now. I still sit and watch them on the telly with my two boys and want them to win. Maybe if there was a big important qualifying game I might go but to watch Bosnia and the like, just out of the question. It's not just that, it costs a fortune now. I've been running the Rangers bus since 1981 and that takes up a lot of my time and money. I can't think of anyone on our bus who goes to watch Scotland.

Peter MacDonald

There's so many rubbish games these days in the qualifiers. I mean Estonia or Bosnia are not going to get you excited, are they? These teams haven't got the big names that used to attract fans to the games. In fact, you'd be hard pushed now to fill a stadium for a Scotland game. Remember, Ibrox wasn't filled a few years ago for the Italy game. I think only Brazil or England could get you a full house now. The Scotland team has a lot to do with it as well. It's full of second rate Englishmen like Sullivan and Elliot and second rate players like Jackson, and Derek Whyte. Derek Whyte for Christ's sake, come on, who are we kidding? And it's not only that, they

93

expect you pay top dollar to watch it. No, I just settle for the television.

Brian Donaghy

On my supporter's bus these days there's a lot of youngsters and they don't show an interest. I've not been for a wee while. There's a lot of apathy now and it costs a lot of money to follow two teams.

Craig Knox

You don't get the same atmosphere, the same buzz as you did years ago in the time of Souness and Dalglish and those kind of players. The younger ones who go to see Scotland now don't know what it was like. . . watching Belarus and Estonia. I mean, they're not Brazil are they.

Alan Smith

Are you joking, go to see Scotland? Do you know how much my season ticket is at Ibrox? It's bad enough watching

Rangers at times far less Scotland. To be honest, apart from the cost, they're very boring. They don't get hammered but they're boring to watch. Craig Brown's got them well organised but I wouldn't pay to watch them.

Alan Park

I wouldn't go to see Scotland now, they are too boring and I certainly wouldn't pay those prices for such low quality football.

John Frame,

I ended up disillusioned with Scotland, I mean you feel a wee bit embarrassed when we qualify for the major championships. We're just not very good.

ALTHOUGH there are still a number of Scottish patriots amongst the Ibrox faithful, it is unlikely that Rangers fans will ever again make up the bulk of the national team's support. Certainly there are no moves from within the ranks of the club or fans to build any bridges. David Murray has made clear his disdain for international football *per se* and is currently seeking a solution to the problem that Rangers have with their players held hostage to the calendar of international matches.[9] Indeed, Scottish football as a whole, with its reliance on overseas players, faces a problem with so many of them often unavailable due to international call-ups.[10] In the meantime clubs are set to pursue a proposal which emanated from ex-Celtic owner Fergus McCann in the mid 1990s when he called for the SFA to compensate clubs for the use of their players. At first this idea was met with derision but gradually, as a business ethos in football has become increasingly dominant, the proposal has gained credibility. A power struggle between clubs, the SFA and FIFA is in its early stages but is set to continue.

Some of the fans' views on international football are clear. An article in the club's matchday programme, from a 'true supporter living and breathing Rangers FC' claimed, 'I am not really interested in the Scotland team'.[11] The club's weekly newspaper, the *Rangers News* carried another piece from 'The Ranger' which, following a poor Scotland performance noted, 'we are playing a different quality of football at Ibrox nowadays and unfortunately, I see absolutely no scope for improvement in the Scotland set-up'.[12] It is an attitude from within Ibrox that indicates a change in priorities. There is no longer any kudos for Rangers fans to have their heroes represent the national team. Indeed, with the number of foreigners plying their trade at Ibrox, international call-ups are often seen as disruptive to the club's preparation for domestic and European matches which are now deemed more important.

International football gave Scottish fans the chance to see the great players from all over the world compete against their own people. Even up until the early 1970s foreign players were relatively unknown quantities and there was a mystique and sense of glamour around many of these occasions. But with television making the football world a smaller place, fans can watch players from all over the globe play in their domestic leagues and competitions. And if there is currently little excitement about foreign stars then there is even less about the Scots players.

Scotland players were once of the highest quality. Jim Baxter, Jimmy Johnstone and Denis Law could hold their own in any football company. The 1978 World Cup squad had European Cup winners Dalglish and Souness and English league champions Kenny Burns, Archie Gemmill and John Robertson. Also, three players – Souness, Gordon McQueen and Joe Jordan – had each been recently transferred for British record transfer fees.[13]

Nowadays, the quality of Scotland player is much less impressive. Scotland manager Craig Brown, admittedly unable to call on many Old Firm players, has to surf the other SPL teams and lower English leagues to make up a squad. And such is the dearth of talent available that he has been reduced in recent times to playing Englishmen such as Matt Elliot, Jonathan Gould, Neil Sullivan and Don Hutcheson. Although Brown operates within FIFA rules, having players with little or no Scottish background in the national team arguably defeats the purpose of international football.

But it is not only Rangers fans who have drifted away from international football. Amongst the Scottish public in general there has been a decline in interest. Scotland were a well-supported team and even friendly matches up until the 1970s could attract huge crowds to Hampden Park. That is no longer the case. A lack of quality players has also characterised most of Scotland's recent opponents. Political changes in Europe have meant there are now more member countries in UEFA and as a result, qualifying groups for the World Cup and the European Championships have been enlarged. Scotland's opponents in the recent past have been the less than glamorous San Marino, Bosnia, Estonia, and the Faroe Islands. Scotland's play-off games against England in 1999 not surprisingly attracted massive interest but in normal circumstances Scotland matches are met with a great deal of apathy. The important European championship qualifier in October 1999 against Bosnia at Ibrox attracted only 30,500 and had one newspaper trying to explain, 'Why we don't back our boys anymore'.[14]

Poor crowds in the recent past have been, in part, disguised by playing games in places like Aberdeen, Edinburgh and Kilmarnock. However, a refurbished Hampden, holding 50,000, will host all Scotland's matches from now on. This may prove to be embarrassing for the SFA as low attendances will highlight the idea that international football is now an idea past its sell-by date.[15] For many Rangers fans, it will be no great loss.

5

Money in the Game

BEING a Rangers fan nowadays is a costly business. But that wasn't always the case because although money has always played an important part in the game, until relatively recently, football was not an expensive hobby. The making of money from fans, and other sources, was not the club's *raison d'etre*.

For the first hundred years of its existence Rangers FC's income came mainly from gate receipts, supplemented since the early sixties by money from the Pools Promoters Association.[1]

Players wages were not a contentious issue, although in the postwar years Ibrox stars were anything but poor relations. Throughout the 1950s Rangers players were well-paid relative to the rest of Britain's footballers. Ian McColl, ex-Rangers and Scotland player and ex-Scotland manager, claimed that in his latter years at Ibrox he earned around £60 a week, 'which was around three times what English players, like Mathews, Mortenson and Finney were on'.[2]

Rangers relied on the success and charisma of the club not only to entice players to Ibrox but also to keep them there. But the ending of the minimum wage in England in the early 60s meant big money could be made down South and many famous Scots players like Bremner and Law by-passed Scottish football for lucrative careers in England. Consequently, throughout the 60s, 70s and early 80s some players at Rangers, aware of their earning potential, regularly complained about their relatively low wages.

According to Ibrox legend Jim Baxter, he wanted to play for Rangers , 'but they were insulting me all the time offering wages which were scandalous. I played for the Rest of the World team in 1963 and I was getting £35. I was ashamed to tell people about that – a team as big as Rangers and me on £35 a week'.[3] Derek Johnstone also noted that wages in the mid-70s were a problem, 'Much as they were a great club, they weren't the greatest payers. It's very different now'.[4] And Gordon Smith claimed that at the time of his move in the early 80s to Brighton, hardly the most glamorous team in the world, they had offered to double his Ibrox wages.[5]

Rangers' reluctance to match the high wages in England must be recognised in the context of the wider Scottish game which traditionally was unwilling to embrace 'proper' marketing techniques and exploit commercial opportunities. The game has changed since 1973 when Celtic chairman Desmond White, some would say with with remarkable foresight, opposed live radio broadcast of a Scottish Cup semi final arguing that Scottish football, 'must not pander to the lazy and indifferent and encourage an armchair audience'.[6]

Maximising revenue from television was simply not an all-consuming passion. Indeed the thought of televising live games on a regular basis was anathema to the Scottish football authorities. In the current climate of live televised football literally seven days a week, it may amuse young supporters to learn that in the early 1970s only twenty minutes of highlights were allowed on a Saturday night[7] and in the season when Rangers won the inaugural Premier League Championship (1975/76), the BBC were paying a mere £550 for each of its 34 recordings per season.[8] However, despite the limited intrusion of television at that time, there were still fears of its consequences and one football journalist warned, 'the box can kill football as we know it'.[9]

Sponsorship of clubs and competitions, crucial in present-day football, was also slow to take a grip on the game. In the 1970s, amidst a storm of controversy, Hibernian broke the mould of nearly a century by having their shirts sponsored by sportswear firm Bukta – then found themselves blanked by television companies who were not sure how to handle the prospect of free advertising.[10] But the Edinburgh club had started a trend, and although the Old Firm had to wait until the 80s for a joint sponsor, shirt sponsorship nowadays plays a crucial part of most top clubs' income.

It wasn't until season 1985/86 that the league had its first ever sponsor, Finefare, the Scottish food chain. At the beginning of that season every Premier League team received the welcome sum of £10,000, first division teams £3000 and the rest £2000.[11] The authorities were beginning to warm to the concept of sponsorship and subsequently, with varying degrees of success, every league and cup competition would seek a backer.

But for Rangers fans, and indeed most supporters, football continued to be relatively inexpensive and sponsorship, broadcasting rights, commercialisation and marketing were terms seldom heard on the terracings.

Stuart Daniels

In the late 50s I began watching Rangers and I remember going to the Co-op for my scarf – it was two and a tanner. They were woollen scarves and they meant everything to you and they brought out silk ones. That was the toffs who wore them. The *Evening Citizen*, you could cut souvenir pictures out of that. Football was a working class sport, but those days are all gone now.

Mike Watt

When I started going to the games you couldn't even buy a replica kit, which was around 1968. You just had the guys outside the ground just like now with pennants, hats and scarves, but that was all really. When I went to Barcelona in 1972, my mates and me went with Cross Travel from Glasgow, so a train down from Aberdeen, then an aeroplane to Spain, accommodation on the night of the game and a match ticket. £35 the lot.

John Frame

I remember going to the 1969 Scottish Cup final and the ticket cost me seven and a tanner and the train fare from the East was around the same. Nobody had replica shirts at that time. It was mainly scarves and programmes you bought and there was the vendors outside the ground who sold scarves and badges.

Jim Black

The first game I was at was in the 60s and my cousin and I were lifted over and put down at the front of the crowd. At half time my dad brought us down an apple each – there was none of your bluenose burgers or pakora then. . . you got the guys outside with the badges and even rosettes but nobody thought of replica kits or anything like that. We got home-made stuff like hats with great big pompoms on the top and ten foot scarves your granny knitted for you.

Colin Glass

I remember buying one of those inflatable Rangers players for £1 in 1971. I thought it was brilliant. It had number 12 on the back of it, same as Derek Johnstone on the day he equalised in the Scottish Cup final. I remember loads of fans kissing it on the train back to the Central station after the game. I also remember that the quarter final tie ticket against Aberdeen cost 30p. Footballers were perceived as being well paid then, and they were relative to the rest of us. But they were not grudged their rewards the way they are now, where mediocre prima donnas are now being paid obscene amounts of money.

Craig Knox

When I started going it cost £1 for a juvenile to get into Ibrox. I know you wouldn't believe it, and that was in the late 70s. I remember, because a pal of mine used to do the Rangers pools and he got 50 pence vouchers, and so two of them and you were in. So more often than not he had enough vouchers to make sure the two of us got in for nothing. At that time all you could get to eat was a pie and a bovril and maybe a macaroon bar from the guy who walked about the crowd. Programmes and scarves were about all you could buy, not like now. I also remember the first Rangers video, *Follow Follow*, you could get it on Beetamax. I thought it was great at the time. Look at it now, you get a video every other month and you've got Rangers television.

Dougie Brown

Looking back it was strange in a way, fans weren't clamouring for all the gear that they can get now. It was a big deal when Rangers changed to the round neck collar in the late 60s, but I can't remember many replica strips at the games, certainly not like now. No way. Things like corporate hospitality weren't even thought of amongst the Rangers fans. Even season tickets, you always thought that only the rich people in the main stand had season tickets. I suppose it's just like mortgages nowadays, with easy credit you can get anything. Mind you, I never paid into a game until I was a teenager – you always got a 'lift over' by your dad or by any passing stranger. It was a bit of psychology I suppose trying to guess who would lift you over. You had to try and ask just at the turnstile so they were more likely to say okay. 'Any chance of a lift o'er mister,' you would say. Try it now and you would get lifted.

Derek McAvoy

I remember when I was younger queuing to pay my season ticket. That's when it was for a section and not for a particular seat. When Ibrox was being reconstructed in the early 80s, the crowds were quite low.

Alan Park

I was a youngster in the late 70s when I first started going to Ibrox and I could pay myself in with my money from my paper round. Into the ground, drinks, sweets. It was different of course then, you had no mass market for all the Rangers gear, children weren't pestering their mums and dads for strips. There was no Rangers shops or souvenir shops. If you wanted something you went to the sports shops in Glasgow, like Greaves.

Charlie McIntyre

I used to go before Souness when you could pay at the gate. The season he arrived there was only a few league games to go and at the last one at Ibrox they were handing out leaflets for season tickets and that's when I got mine. At that time they never knew their full commercial potential. I mean they had that silly wee souvenir shop across from the Stadium bar.

Ian Campbell

It was the early 80s, about '81 when I first started going up to Ibrox and I could get in the boys gate for £1.25. You didn't have all that Rangers Direct stuff then. My mum got my Rangers duvet from Hawick Market.

Peter McFarlane

I remember the Torino game the season Rangers won the Cup Winner's Cup. My parents were skint and the only way I could get the bus fare was taking a hundred Embassy coupons to the newsagents where you got cash for them. I was so embarrassed, I walked about two miles out of my way in case I bumped into my mates. I wasn't bothered about getting in, I could always manage to get a lift over, but Ibrox was too long a walk. I skipped my bus fare that night and had enough to buy my first programme. It would be some bus journey now that would cost the price of a Rangers programme.

WHEN FOOTBALL became fashionable again in the early 90s Rangers were already geared up to meet the challenge of a new football culture. Tragic circumstances dictated that Rangers would have a head start over the rest of Scottish (and British) football in terms of updating and revamping the facilities enjoyed by the fans. The Ibrox disaster in 1971 when sixty six fans lost their lives, prompted Rangers, eventually, to refurbish the antiquated stadium. Although the Centenary stand had been opened in 1973, it had amounted to little more than removing crush barriers and replacing them with benches. The real work on the stadium had begun in 1978 and when completed in 1983, Ibrox had a reduced capacity of 44,000 with 36,000 seated. Further alterations and additions were implemented throughout the 90s.

A similar disaster eighteen years later would force the rest of British football to follow suit. The tragedy at Hillsborough in 1989, when ninety six Liverpool fans lost their lives, shamed the football authorities and clubs into action and after a subsequent investigation, the Taylor Report meant that clubs had to upgrade their facilities at great expense. Ibrox, almost unaffected by Taylor's guidelines, was held up as a, 'model of ground redevelopment offering good facilities at reasonable prices'.[12]

By that time Rangers had overcome something of a crisis in the club's history. Providing evidence that results and not facilities are crucial to attendances, Rangers underperformed in the early to mid 80s and average crowds were around 25,000 with some individual gates much lower. Incredibly, given present day trends, only 2,600 of the fans were season ticket holders.[13] Although a modern stadium would provide a base for Rangers to find success, it was changes in personnel that would improve the fortunes of the club.

When David Holmes came in at the behest of Lawrence Marlborough in 1985, there was little indication that Rangers FC was set to fundamentally restructure itself. Marlborough, based in America, had taken control after a power struggle and quickly had in place three of his own men, Holmes, Hugh Adam and Freddy Fletcher. Their remit was simple – to make Rangers a financially viable organisation. Significantly, none of the new recruits were Rangers supporters, thus a more dispassionate and businesslike approach was implemented.[14]

Holmes' first six months was low key as he took stock of the situation he had inherited. It was only when he brought Graeme Souness to Ibrox in 1986 that the Ibrox fans, and the rest of British football, sat up and took notice.

Souness quickly reversed Rangers' frugal fiscal policies which in the recent past had lost the Ibrox club their captain John McClelland (to Watford) and Gordon Smith (to Brighton). The record signing had been £235,000 – Craig Paterson from Hibs – and no player earned more than £240 per week. But Souness moved quickly to smash the record transfer fee for a goalkeeper when he bought in Chris Woods from Norwich for £600,000 and many more players quickly followed including high profile England internationalists like Terry Butcher and Graham Roberts.[15]

Souness's signings shattered the egalitarian wage structure at Ibrox and his largesse with Rangers' money became legendary. Dave McPherson was suitably shocked in wage negotiation when offered four times more than he was going to initially demand. Not all players benefited but the Ibrox gold rush was accepted by those who never quite staked the same claim.[16] It was then that the die was cast for the future in terms of the individual wage bargaining between club and players.

It was a classic case of speculating to accumulate. Home gates soared up to around 39,000 in 1988 as fans flocked back to witness the Souness revolution. Financial spin-off ensued and Fletcher had increased commercial revenue from £239,000 in 1985/86 to £2.2m by 1987/88.[17] David Murray's takeover of the club in 1988 served simply to move Rangers up to a higher level. Murray had come in with a brilliant business background and his maximisation of executive facilities, office space and sponsorship meant that by the end of the 80s, 'only 30% of the club's total income was generated by gate receipts.[18] It was an incredibly successful business 'make over' which other clubs could only look at with envy.

Paradoxically, the footballing revolution at Ibrox occurred at a time when British football as a whole was at an all-time low. The problems of hooliganism, although more widespread in England, provoked the Government into responding with threats of identity cards and bans on away fans. For different reasons, the disasters of Heysel and Hillsborough had left football reeling and the average football fan was treated as a social outcast. However, amidst all this chaos, Rangers were thriving. Flynn and Guest best summed up Rangers progress by the late 1980s, noting that 'they had become a prime example of the failure of the English game to keep up with the rest of the world. . . despite their protestations, the big English clubs cannot even challenge for the title of the biggest club in Britain. That title now belongs to Glasgow Rangers'.[19]

The new Ibrox ethos of big money signings, funded by expanding commercial activities and new marketing techniques, was recognised by most of the Ibrox faithful as necessary to restore Rangers FC to their former glories. An academic study carried out on Rangers fans in 1990 reported that in terms of the Ibrox club's attitude to commercialism, 81% of fans thought that Rangers had the balance just about right.[20] The survey also noted that, in contrast to the views of fans of English teams, there were, 'remarkably high levels of satisfaction exhibited by Rangers fans about the way their own club treats and provides for them'.[21] Thus, at the beginning of the 1990s, with the Ibrox revolution well under way, in the eyes of most fans, Rangers could do no wrong.

Alan Park

When Souness came we felt we were ready to take on the world, the money was obviously there to play with. For all the big money they paid for the like of Butcher and Roberts they got their money's worth. These guys were obviously professionals but they played for the jersey and the fans recognised that. It was when the foreigners came that the fans got upset about the money aspect.

Charlie McIntyre

The whole Souness thing was brilliant at the time. We were buying the captain of England and other established England internationals. Butcher was rumoured to have knocked back Man United and Spurs to come up here. Rangers fans were all walking around as proud as punch. But now we're paying the price for a decade of bad buying, no money in the bank now, I mean we can't even go that wee bit extra of £500,000 to get Paul Ritchie.

John Frame

I had been following Rangers through the bad times and all of a sudden, when Souness came, I couldn't get a ticket for the games. That's why I had to buy a season ticket. There is no doubt a lot of people just jumped on the bandwagon at that time but I wasn't too bothered to be honest. For years English teams had raided Scotland for our best players and now were doing it to them . . . I didn't think too much about the wages they were on at that time. We had to pay for the best and that's what we were doing.

Gordon Inglis

Just before Souness you would watch Rangers playing and there would be empty spaces on the terraces, but then there was a sudden surge in interest and we were getting locked out of grounds like Dunfermline. . . It was obvious that Butcher and company were getting wages which were a step up from the normal Ibrox level but we accepted that.

Peter Macfarlane

I have to admit at the time of Souness, most Rangers fans were gloating at the big money buys we could afford and how we were leaving the rest of Scottish football behind. We didn't really realise that eventually it would start costing us a bomb to finance it all.

Every other week it was this big name player and that big name player and all the Celtic fans were squirming. They used to say, 'I don't care, Scottish football's shite.' Then when they started buying big salaried players and they eventually won it a few years ago, suddenly it was worth winning and they were dancing in the streets.

Rhys Jones

For the first time Rangers could afford to attract big name players, international players of world renown. This signified how big the Ibrox board's plans were. . . it never bothered me how much these players got as long as they put the graft in on the pitch. That's still the way I feel now.

Stuart Daniels

Well, Souness broke the wage structure. He was a mercenary. I felt the players he brought in got paid in excess even at that time, but it was inevitable that Rangers went down that road.

AT THE BEGINNING of the 1990s, British football became fashionable again. A relatively successful England World Cup campaign in Italia 90 and the emergence of satellite television, were two factors in a cultural revolution which attracted a new 'breed' of fan to the game.

Rangers, in many ways the pioneers of the commercial age, were well placed to tap into the new interest in the game and their commercial operations, driven by onfield success, went into overdrive. However, amongst the Ibrox faithful, there slowly developed an unease about the way the club were determined to maximise their earning potential. A bond scheme was introduced in March 1990, costing the fans between £1000 and £1650. Purchasers got a lifetime right to buy a season ticket in the new top deck which was added to the Main Stand in 1992.[22] Many fans wondered why the simple task of renewing their ticket every season didn't give you the same guarantee. In 1995 supporters were asked to fork out on a £399 'Ready for the Future' scheme which allowed them to buy the right to season tickets for the next twenty five years.[23]

The Rangers crest was on everything from chocolate to clothes, from champagne to jewellery. Club shops opened up in Glasgow and Belfast and in 1996 a Superstore was added to the ground itself. By 1997 the commercial side of Rangers' income, made up of corporate hospitality, sponsorship, advertising and merchandising was claimed to account for 43p in every pound.[24]

There was the introduction of the 'beamback' – live away games transmitted to giant screens erected in the corners of Ibrox. And Rangers introduced a glossy monthly magazine in 1998 to supplement their weekly newspaper. The magazine was professionally produced and included several interesting new ideas but the commercial aspect of it shone through. A premium rate phone number was used in a 'competition' to win a replica home kit. In order to maximise profits from this 'hotline', potential callers were directed to the answers elsewhere in the magazine![25] In June 1999 there was also an opportunity for fans to be photographed in the club shop with the three domestic trophies Rangers had won the previous season. The cost was a staggering £15 and to add insult to injury, no personal cameras were allowed in the store.

There seemed no end to the way in which money was made off the backs of the fans. A competition was initiated by the club to find the 'Greatest Ranger' and the 'Greatest Rangers team'. This idea was ostensibly a bit of fun which would end, or begin, arguments amongst the fans as to who were the best Rangers players of all time. However, the idea was felt to be sullied when competition voters were sent leaflets exhorting them to buy a video and book of the event.

It was all getting a bit much for Rangers fans and indeed all football supporters, who began to feel commercialism was becoming the dominant feature of football. When the Office of Fair Trading reported that football supporters were being ripped off by the price fixing of replica strips, they made official only what most fans had come to accept as fact. Umbro and Nike had restricted supermarket chains from offering discounted prices on £60 strips that had been made for considerably less. Umbro, makers of the Celtic kit, pompously claimed that they did not want their merchandise sold beside baked beans and then embarrassingly awaited the return of 30,000 Celtic strips which were falling apart through poor workmanship and substandard materials.[26]

Although many Rangers fans gloated at the negative publicity the strip debacle generated for their rivals, they too have been manipulated and exploited in terms of merchandising. And over the years it has become more subtle and cynical. Rangers traditional red, white and blue have been slowly ousted as the dominant club colours. When Rangers players celebrated their league win back at Ibrox at the end of season 1998/99 many of them had new and unfamiliar light and dark blue scarves around their necks. It was a clever, if cynical marketing ploy to get the fans accustomed to those colours which would adorn not only the following season's new away strip but countless other items of merchandise.

The 1999 Rangers official merchandise catalogue confirmed this theory. Sky blue and dark blue were 'this seasons colours', dominating the new range of caps, holdalls, t-shirts, tracksuits and rain jackets.[27] It was a tax on the loyalty of Rangers supporters but unsurprisingly, many fans still paraded the colours more befitting Manchester City or Coventry. Another two financially fruitful colours had been added to the countless marketing combinations already in place using the more traditional blue, red, white, black, and orange.

But perhaps the commercial nadir was when the fans were asked to buy a Commerative Brick for £35 in order to help the club build a new training and development centre. The scheme was launched at a time when the squandering of money at Ibrox had never been more conspicuous. Players like Marco Negri were continuing to pick up a fortune in wages without contributing, Daniel Prodan had returned to his homeland still to make his debut for Rangers, and short term signing Colin Hendry had been sold to Coventry City, almost inevitably, at a loss of millions of pounds.[28]

In mitigation, Rangers have only reacted to the changing face of football and it would be silly to think they could somehow operate outside the commercial mania of the modern game. But although the Ibrox club were not the only ones to go down the commercial road, they have been arguably the most innovative. Where they led, other clubs followed. In the late 80s that would have been taken as a compliment – now it can be construed as criticism. All football fans continually press their club's boards to find new ways of making money and Rangers fans would have been no different – if the club had not continually been one step in front of them.

Obviously, fans are not obliged to buy all the Rangers merchandise or take part in their ventures but there is felt to exist an element of emotional blackmail in all the commercial ideas and concepts. The club has always been quick to point out that monies from the fans were going to pay for the top players to come to Rangers. And this boast was true to an extent. David Murray has provided Rangers with a conveyor belt of new players. But through no fault of his own, he found that generally, the best players wouldn't come to Scottish football. As Rangers failed in Europe year after year, a situation arose where attitudes towards the highly paid Ibrox players changed.

When Souness brought in top quality players there was little grumbling amongst the fans about the wage bill at Ibrox or the money spent on transfer fees. Post-Bosman, attitudes have changed.

The infamous 'Bosman ruling' ensued after the court case involving Belgian footballer Jean Marc Bosman and meant that players were free to leave their clubs when their contract was finished. This freedom of movement which 'normal' workers all over the Europe enjoyed, added to the financial 'overheating' that was already taking place in football. PFA chairman Tony Higgins asserted that, 'Bosman was always a poisoned chalice – the top ten percent in the game are earning far more that they ever did but as a consequence of that, monies that were dispersed further down the line have disappeared'.[29]

What quickly emerged from the Bosman ruling was the phenomenon of player power and it arrived in Scotland in the shape of Celtic's Jorge Cadette, Pierre van Hoijdoonk and Paolo di Canio. The Celtic stars had various problems, all financial, which initially amused Ibrox fans until their very own sullen Italian, Marco Negri, was bitten by the same bug. However, unlike Celtic, who found buyers for their distressed players, no club was willing to match the wages Negri was 'earning'. The chickens had come home to roost for Rangers in terms of their inflated salary structures. Negri's situation was the clearest indication that Ibrox had become a footballing utopia.

Squandering money is a habit that some feel has been indulged since the Souness era. Non-Rangers fans, increasingly unimpressed with the Ibrox club's domestic success, laughed at the money spent on players such as Oleg Kutznetsov(£1.4m) and Basile Boli (£2.7m) and even Rangers fans gasped at the sense of desperation in some signings, none more so than in the cases of Lorenzo Amaruso and Daniel Prodan (£2.2m) who both arrived at Ibrox carrying serious injuries.

Throughout this time, fans were constantly reminded that in order to compete for the top players, ticket prices would have to increase. Paradoxically, when fans complained about the increases, they were then told that such was the revenue stream from other sources, their money in fact didn't keep the club afloat at all. Reluctantly, most Ibrox fans, still nursing the European dream, continued to pay the increased costs of their football. However, in season 1999/2000 there was serious rumblings of discontent amongst the fans as a massive hike in season book prices threatened to cause irreparable damage between club and supporters.

Mike Watt

My ticket in the West Enclosure went up £55 this season to £355, well over the top. The planning was terrible, saying you wouldn't get Scottish Cup ties either. They keep bandying about this 10,000 waiting list but that's a lot of rubbish. They're just trying to frighten you into putting up with their increases. There was a couple of guys on my bus last year who went to every game, home and away and this season they just stopped, they couldn't afford it anymore. Same as those bond ideas asking you to pay upwards of £1000 to guarantee your seat. The way I look at it is as long as I don't misbehave and pay my ticket every year then that is a guaranteed ticket for life. The same as that name a seat thing. They've had a few ideas like that but that was another rip off. Every avenue, they want to milk it, it's ridiculous. Then they try and flog you a car park space for over £200, it's money all the time. Do you know my daughter took her car there and it cost her £7.50 for a couple of hours.

Alan Park

The rover tickets in the mid 80s were around £120 as far as I can remember. My seat this season in the Copland Road end is up £50 to £270. Far too much of an increase. Some of the stuff I'm not happy about, I mean that monthly magazine, that's just nonsense. I never buy it. Funny enough our membership on our bus is up this season but punters are picking and choosing their games unlike previous seasons when we had a lower membership but they were there every week.

Charlie McIntyre

To be honest this season, I halved my season ticket with a mate. There's four of us and we've got two season tickets between us. My ticket in the club deck went up £80, absolutely ridiculous – that took it up to £470. And that's not all – last season we could park in the carpark for £2, this season it went up to £7. They also had the cheek to try and sell season tickets for the carpark which would cost you double what it would cost on a game by game basis. Three or four years ago I would say there was about twenty season ticket holders from Campbeltown that I knew of, now there's only about nine. It's the whole take-it-or-leave-it attitude that gets me. I phoned up Ibrox for a favour to help out a sick friend of mine and just got shunted from pillar to post and nobody replied to my letters. It seems as if it is a case of take it or leave it.

Derek McAvoy

The price of season tickets are excessive, especially as Rangers do not play a high quality of opposition. This season David Murray put up the price of my ticket by £50 and also withdrew Scottish Cup games. Many people have not renewed and unless he changes this 'take the piss out of the fans' policy Rangers may be struggling to fill Ibrox in ten years time. People will chose their games and not go to the minor ones.

Ian Campbell

It's a carry-on now. They just want you to buy all their stuff out of the Rangers shop, get in the ground and buy their burgers and pies. David Murray, ranting and raving to get your money in and having the nerve to ask for debentures. It's now about maximising profits and basically taking advantage of the fans. It's got too much. This season me and my mate went halfers on a season ticket. The price went up from £365 to £425. I know people who went home and away over the last three years or so and they're not going anymore. On our minibus there are about 7 or 8 regulars and the rest rotate, people maybe going every third game or whatever. It's apparently the same in the Hawick club, they've got 25 regulars and the rest rotate. Rangers don't seem to realise there is a lot of unemployment down here in the Borders and those who are working are not all getting great money. Even if I watch my money it will cost £40 to go to a game.

Derek Inglis

I don't like the way they shove the Rangers Direct thing down your throat. It's just like begging. I think Rangers fans know by now not to go to other sports shops to buy their stuff.

John Frame

In 1994 my season ticket was £206, this season it was up at £310 and I was angry at that. It could be worse because I'm a club 2000 member which entitles me to ten percent off, but that's due to run out shortly. David Murray talks about buying Rangers Direct. I think that's a little bit of emotional blackmail. I certainly wouldn't buy the replica shirts again at £40 a time. I can get three or four polo tops for that. The thing about the players at Ibrox now, especially the ones who can't get in the team, is that they have golden handcuffs. They are paid so much that other teams can't afford to pay their wages even if they get them for nothing.

Brian Whitelaw

There is always a cost of course. We expect success now, so we have to bring in so many foreign players. This costs us big bucks and also harms the progress of local players. However, most of us will accept this if it means we win trebles and do well in Europe.

Gordon Inglis

I never really think, 'Oh there's a guy getting twenty or forty grand a week.' The players at the moment all seem to be playing for the club, and like all companies, if someone is going to pay you that kind of money you'll take it. But people like Negri, who rip the piss out of it, get on everybody's nerves.

Ian McColl

Scott Symon said to me when I was the Scottish manager that some time in the future Rangers players of my quality, when they're finished playing, would never need to work again. And it's here. That's the way football has gone.

Jim Black

The kind of the money guys like Kanchelskis gets – he's hardly kicked a ball – to me he's not interested. Clubs should be run like businesses – they should be able to say, look, you're not performing, we'll have to look at this contract and perhaps say, I'm afraid we'll have to terminate it. As it is players at Ibrox are in a no-lose situation. Over the years the prices of season tickets have went up a tenner here and a tenner there but this season was the biggest increase yet. I was at the Supporter's Association's AGM and Campbell Ogilvie said that in the next couple of years or so, prices will not go up more than eight per cent. I asked him if Mr Murray knew what the rate of inflation was and that if workers could negotiate an eight per cent rise every year they would have won a watch. Our supporters club gives some guys an interest free loan to buy their season tickets, otherwise they would struggle.

Stuart Daniels

It used to be football players trying to be stars, nowadays it's stars trying to be football players. . . you hear about all these thigh strains and hamstrings and everything – they're never injured when they go to the cashline, they seem to have marching bandsmen's feet when they go to the cashline. They paid a premium for Negri, for Hendry and other players. It was the Lewis money that came into Ibrox, the £40m, they went daft on that. Prodan, Rozental, I mean what are these players still getting paid? I never renewed my season ticket this season and it broke my heart. Just on a point of principle. The Govan front went up from £295 to £365. If my season book's £500 and I can't pay that up front in May then I can pay four payments of £150 spread over the year, but that takes it up to £600! The commercial side is over the top especially that idea of opening up a shop at Glasgow Airport, that wasn't fair. You get families going holidays and they are on a budget and kids being kids, they'll want some gear. They were just money making machines, I was glad when Glasgow Airport knocked them back.

Rhys Jones

A day trip to Ibrox is a very pricey thing these days. Our supporter's club travels around once a month and that entails a 5 o'clock start and we don't get home until about 10.30 at night, so it's a long day. The ticket and travel alone costs around £60 and you still have to eat, perhaps have a drink and I usually buy something for my wee girl. The stuff in the Rangers shop is good quality but it is a wee bit pricey. So all in all, it could cost around £120 for the whole day. I'd love to go more often but it's not fair on my family, the kids are growing up and they need things.

John MacMillan

The issue of cost has had an effect on the fans. The ones who don't have season tickets are picking and choosing their games now. For example there is a definite trend away from League Cup ties, there is no doubt about that. It is good for the prestige of the club but basically it's about money and Europe is where all the big money is. I'll tell you now, Sky will sooner or later pull the plug on the types of game such as Dundee versus Kilmarnock, with all due respect to them, because the viewing figures will be so low. No television company is going to pay any sort of money to have cameras panning round empty stadiums. The product in Scotland is not good enough for them to continue

their sponsorship. They are only interested in Rangers and Celtic. I don't think TV is doing the fans a favour, there is plenty of money in the club's coffers at the moment but come a few years time they may rue the day they ever signed that contract. I'm on record to David Murray as saying if TV decides to pull the plug, and that could happen, where do we go from there? Fans are tending to stay at home and watch the games on TV. . . I told David Murray, football has sold its soul. Fans cannot go to two games a week. It's bad enough if you are a fan on your own but if you have a youngster or two youngsters, then the expense multiplies. If Rangers hadn't qualified for the group stage of the Champions League this season they were going to charge £25 for UEFA Cup tickets. Well if anyone had come on to me to ask for my views, I would have slated that policy.

Anthony Orr

I don't think football has the capacity or fanbase to continue growing at the rate it has. Once the middle classes lose interest, and they will, ticket prices and corporate hospitality will be under pressure, as will paying the wages.

HOW MUCH longer will the Ibrox fans continue to pay the escalating price of being a fan? To an extent it all relies on the current fashion for football to continue. Ticket prices are probably as high as the club can set them without inviting further adverse reactions. The club look to have drawn the same conclusion with their announcement in April 2000 of a modest reduction in the cost of season ticket books. In terms of merchandise, then the simple business practice of supply and demand dictate that if fans can't afford or don't want football 'gear' then they won't buy it. In the case of replica tops, which have become a fashion accessory as much as a show of support, there will undoubtedly be an end to the 'craze'. Fashion is driven by change, and in a few years time no doubt it will be decidedly uncool to wear a replica Rangers shirt. In the meantime, the ill-feeling that was generated in the 1999/00 season when the club brought out a costly, predominantly white/sky blue away strip, then seldom wore it, certainly won't encourage future sales.

The other marketing and commercial activities – the corporate boxes, catering, sponsorship and club shops – will continue to be important but those resources have proved insufficient in providing Rangers with the revenue needed to reach the top in European terms. The Ibrox club now requires a whole new level of funding in order to allow it to compete at the very highest level – and increased television revenue may be the answer.

Pay-per-view, the message goes, is the future for football, a venture which will bring untold millions into the coffers of the top clubs. Management consultant David Low claimed, 'we are approaching the age of the virtual supporter, where fans will follow their club without ever visiting a football ground. Once clubs own their own TV rights, and that will come sooner rather than later, it will really take off'.[30]

What would happen in Scotland if teams were freed of all-inclusive television deals such as the present Sky arrangement and could sell their own matches? Some of the smaller clubs would be unlikely to broker any kind of meaningful deal themselves and would be left to look for compensation from those opponents who could command an audience. Let's say Rangers were playing Motherwell at Ibrox. Would the money Rangers received from selling that game be enough to compensate their opponents for no longer being involved in an all-League agreement. With the big clubs at present refusing to split their home gate money, in the long run, any democratic notions seem unlikely. But if no money was forthcoming would Motherwell refuse to play?

Given the boredom and monotony that characterises many Rangers games, especially at Ibrox, would anyone suggest that armchair fans are going to pay even £5 to watch a normal Rangers league match? Of course the overseas market is where a lot of the new technological developments like pay-per-view and the Internet are aimed. But although there are many ex-pats who support Rangers in countries like Canada, America and Australia, it is only speculation to claim they will all be rushing to partake in any kind of television season ticket.

In Holland, the top three teams, Ajax, PSV and Feyenoord, won individual television rights and then found that the other Dutch clubs refused to play them, a snub from which the concept of the Atlantic League was born. This is the central issue that people who claim football is a business cannot seem to comprehend. You need opposition to play against. In 'normal' business practice, there's plenty of good reasons for closing down all your competitors. In football it's futile.

Any thoughts that a pay-per-view scheme would be successful in a European football context must also be challenged. To have any chance of this idea being viable,

Rangers would have to make progress in the Champions League every year. Failure in the early stages would demote Rangers to the UEFA Cup, playing, for the most part, unattractive sides – a problem which any proposed form of Atlantic or Euro League would also pose.

But the issue of the connection between television and football will not go away. Media groups are gearing up to buy into the clubs and this development should not be taken lightly. According to Hearts chief executive Chris Robinson, the biggest day in the club's history was not winning any trophy, but the investment by the Scottish Media Group of £8 million.[31] Significantly, SMG were able to appoint a director of their own choice onto the Hearts board. The SMG investment mirrored such developments as Granada's move into Liverpool and BskyB's move into Leeds United.

SPFA Chairman Tony Higgins has his own fears of the impending media buy-out of clubs. He claims, 'The problem of media investment is that the next time there is a crisis the media buy more of you. The worry in the long term is that if the media companies all own the clubs then when it comes to sharing out the cake, or the new deal, then there is a conflict of interests. The directors would not want to talk any TV deal up. So you have to be careful. They could actually underprice football, then sell out to the BBC or someone and make a fortune for themselves. We understand PLCs don't just come in for the good of the game'.[32] Thus, the great irony is that in the long run, football clubs could get less money from television and media companies, rather than more.

6

The Scottish Premier League
and the future

THERE is nothing left for Rangers to achieve in Scottish football. After eleven successes in the last twelve years, winning the Championship offers no honour, no glory and no credibility – the accomplishment brings only a sense of relief. The domestic Cup competitions offer nothing more than an uninspiring series of potential embarrassments. On a subconscious level, at least, the Ibrox fans seem to realise this predicament.

The recent Ibrox domination of Scottish football has consequently left the Rangers fans bloated with success and harder to please than ever.[1] Any strangers visiting Ibrox for a normal league match would hardly be inspired by the atmosphere inside the stadium. Matches are not treated as a competitive battle but are looked upon as something of a ritualistic slaughter. The fans turn up a few minutes before kick off and sit in expectant silence waiting for the goals to flood in. The quicker the points are safe, the better, because seemingly, thousands are in a rush to get home. In a ritual which is fast becoming part of Scottish footballing folklore, many fans slip away early, regardless of the score, and the ground is often half full when the final whistle blows. Ibrox can generate a feeling that, for some fans, the matches interrupt their everyday life. It is a home support in the loosest sense of the phrase.

In fact, there are signs that the fans have had enough. There were strong rumours that season ticket sales plummeted before season 1999/2000. Having regained the title from Celtic, the thought of ploughing through another nine titles in a row obviously did not fill the Ibrox fans with eager anticipation. Stories abounded of ticket office staff struggling to recruit from a waiting list, which indeed, many claim to be mythical in terms of its numbers. One fan Davie MacDonald, secretary of the Irvine and District RSC claimed, 'Earlier this season, I just walked in and bought a season ticket for my son and I also bought one for a friend. Some waiting list.'[2] Ominously, Rangers didn't sell out any of their home league games, Celtic apart, in the first part of the 99/00 season.

When Souness came to Ibrox in 1986 there was a genuine sense of excitement and optimism amongst the Rangers fans. Capacity crowds flocked back to Ibrox and their interest and enthusiasm continued as the early novelty of Championship wins turned into the ultimately succesful quest for nine in a row. Ibrox was seldom less than packed for all games.

However, times have changed, not only in terms of trophies won. Supply now looks like exceeding demand. There was a capacity increase at Ibrox which took up a lot of the slack and Murray, perhaps astutely, has ruled out further expansion. Furthermore, season tickets seemed like value for money at around £200 in the exciting 80s and early 90s but with the potential for excitement exhausted, they start to look expensive at nearer £400 in the present day.

Any discussions on the future of football wouldn't be complete without mentioning Sky television, who in the recent past have invested heavily in Scottish football. Unsurprisingly, the Old Firm feature in most of the matches. Rangers performed regularly in the 99/00 season at the 6.05pm Sunday slot, a time which is patently unsuitable for the many Ibrox fans from England and Northern Ireland. Season tickets no longer make sense for the fans who can only manage along to some home games.

Thus, the combination of 'trophy fatigue', high ticket prices, saturation television and the tampering with traditional kick-off times, could be set to herald a downward spiral. There are tickets for sale outside Ibrox at every home match, except Celtic, which will surely encourage more season ticket holders to give up their books and take a chance on a game by game basis. And when people realise they can pick and choose their games, that is exactly what they will do. Without the need to pay in advance, there will be a return to the 'old' days before Souness, when fans could leave it to the last minute before deciding whether they went to the game.

Inevitably, matches against teams like St Johnstone and Motherwell will be spurned by the more discerning supporters and consequently gate income and commercial monies could nose-dive. Ticket prices for the Scottish Cup quarter final tie against Hearts in March 2000 were slashed but still only 31,000 fans turned up, clear evidence that the rot may have set in. This is not a phenomenon peculiar to Rangers. Celtic's nine in a row campaign from 1966-1974 finished with their crowds falling away – and from a much smaller starting point.[3] But if a similar situation arises with Rangers, there will be no way back. Rangers, and indeed football in general, have both had their revolution. The coveted nine in a row has been won and the club may not stand being reinvented again.

A fan's sense of excitement can't be manufactured or turned on like a tap. It has to come from within. There has to be the danger that your team might be beaten and there has to be the feeling that your opponents are credible. How can Rangers fans experience these emotions when other Scottish club's managers and players, Celtic's apart, no longer pretend they can match Rangers and give up the Championship race before the season has started. When there is credible opposition, which is clearly the case on European nights at Ibrox, the self same fans can whip up an incredible atmosphere as was shown in the 1999 matches against Bayern Munich and Parma. But in the run of the mill league games, normal service is resumed.

Stuart Daniels

We're paying for an inferior product. Murray said he was committed to Scottish football. That saddened me. The Premiership, that's where we should be within the next decade because your season book now – the product is two Old Firm games and two grudge games against Aberdeen. That's what I feel you're paying your season book for. Paying more for less – no Scottish Cup ties, that will be extra. Remember the other teams are up for it against Rangers. That's what makes it difficult. I mean, you can get ten midden bins that are organised that can make it difficult. The Scottish Premier League has run its course, the Dundees and Kilmarnocks of this world. People are looking for a better product and they get a taste of it on a European stage. Rangers could do it gradually, keep some sort of team in the Premier league. I mean for years these teams have milked off the Old Firm so it's payback time now, we must leave them behind. . . The prices go up every year. What was it last time? Six times the rate of inflation. It's ridiculous. Football takes up a large part of people's income now and that's the downside of being a bluenose. . . they've moved away from the working class and Rangers don't just want the money out of your pocket, they want the lining. Everything's geared to money – you can get life insurance, car insurance, endowments, credit cards, it's a multi-million pound business. The likes of guys like myself, it's not a sport, it's a way of life. We build our lives around Rangers. It affects our family. I say I can't go there I'll be going to the game. People say 'Stuart, come to a party', and I say I can't go, I'll miss the game. I wonder sometimes, do the players realise what some of the fans go through, sitting doubled up on a bus for three days going abroad for ninety minutes football. The Kanchelskis of this world, I wonder if they realise this. Struth would have chased him along the subway from Copland Road to Cessnock, through the tunnel with a cutlass in his hand! The Ronaldos and the Batistutas of this world will not come to this league, you can only show them Duck Bay Marina so many times. The £40m ENIC money, that's been a tragedy. People leaving with ten minutes to go? It's like going to see Sinatra and before he sings *My Way*, he sees people walking out! He'd be saying, what the hell's going on here.

Julian Brent

I hope they get out of Scottish football. It's no good at all. They're far too big for Scotland. It's pathetic, winning the Championship means winning four matches against Celtic. I

mean how can anyone get excited about playing against St Johnstone? I would take anything except the SPL.

Jim Black

It saddens me when I see the opposing teams that come to Ibrox and pack the defence hoping for a draw. I cannot think of a way to try and stop this as survival is all that counts to these teams. It's not the first time it has been mentioned by my mates who sit beside me that we would be better off in the supporters club having a pint than having to watch what was happening on the park. I have not succumbed so far but I have come mighty close on some occasions.

Charlie McIntyre

I would rather stick with the SPL but I would possibly take it up to sixteen teams. I don't mind going to see your Mother-wells and Hibs but playing each other four times is a wee bit much. To play St Johnstone in the cup as well as four league games, well familiarity breeds contempt. I'd like to see St Mirren, Falkirk, Dunfermline, there's definitely scope for making it sixteen teams. It's all very well saying there's too many easy games for Rangers and Celtic but it will give them a chance to play your Barry Nicholsons and guys like that. You can't get a chance to judge young guys at the moment and we lost a good player in Greg Shields because he never got a chance to see what he can do. And Rangers and Celtic, if they finish above the other, have got as easy a route to the Champions League as any team has in Europe, so what's the problem?

Grant Aitchison

I was up at Aberdeen when Rangers won the league and it's definitely not the same now. But I'm quite happy the way it is alongside the Champions League. I think the standard of football is okay although I prefer the away games. At Ibrox a lot of fans don't back the team. A lot of them just go to say they go to Ibrox. They criticise the team although they may be winning three or four nothing.

Willie Buchan

To be quite honest I don't think the Premier League is that bad. It's nothing great but what can you do? You have to play in your own League. Sometimes the atmosphere isn't what it should be, the supporters don't seem to back the team. I think they're expecting four and five every week and that's the problem. Rangers are expected to go through the whole season undefeated and that's impossible. I prefer the away games, everybody seems to encourage the team away from home.

Gordon Graham

When we look at most of the fare served up on Sky, there is no doubt we have an inferior product, there is no doubt about that, although you do see some rubbish there as well. The Premier League has got to the stage where you go home and away with the exception of Celtic Park and you're expecting to win. I don't think you can call the SPL entertaining. I don't count beating teams 6-0 as entertainment, although a lot of people enjoy that, but it wouldn't entertain a neutral. You have got to say winning the League so often has devalued it but of course I wouldn't like to see anyone else winning it. At the five, six, seven in a row stage you were maybe playing a team like Dundee and you would score after four or five minutes and after that it was dead. I looked around me one time and said to my mate

Davie, they're not interested, they're all talking about where they're going at night, they weren't even watching the game. I don't expect teams like Motherwell to come and play five men in attack and get hammered, but it's this business of ten men behind the ball and some of the teams not even leaving one player up. Even last season when we beat Kilmarnock 5-0 down there, they were challenging at the top end of the table but, Christ almighty, for a home team, the offside trap, defensive tactics, it was ridiculous.

Tanya Orr

The only Rangers Premier League games I enjoy are the Celtic ones as you know at least both teams are going out there to give their all and actually try and win.

Craig Knox

The money you pay for a season ticket it's not really value for money. We have to do some-thing. Look at Hearts just before Christmas at Ibrox defending the whole game and Jim Jeffries is trying to defend the way they played. That says it all. Hearts two seasons ago were pushing us all the way and they expect you to fork out over £300 a season to watch that. I'd rather see Rangers play Anderlecht and Ajax. Okay we might not win all the time but at least you're guaranteed better quality teams who'll make Rangers a better team. Were getting held back in this league we're in and with an Atlantic League you'd get better players.

Alan Park

Rangers can step up to the top level of European competition – we've seen that this season in the games against the likes of Bayern Munich, but the Premier League is stunting our progress. Teams like St Johnstone and Dundee are dragging us down. There's not the real buzz that there was years ago, being really up for the likes of a home game against Aberdeen, which you knew was going to be a really good tight game. Now it's a case of, we're going to Ibrox, we've got Aberdeen, big deal. I don't think there is any way we can improve the quality but I think this playing each other four times a season and maybe a cup tie, like St Johnstone this season, that alone takes the spice out of games.

Dave Taylor

I feel the entertainment value of some of the home games at Ibrox this season has been very poor. Teams come to Ibrox and set out to defend which isn't much fun to watch. I wouldn't say I was bored, I'll never be bored watching Rangers, but it's very disappointing to see a team like Hearts come to Ibrox and defend the whole game. Most times we do break teams down but it isn't always flowing football we see.

Brian Donaghy

The SPL games at Ibrox are not value for money. It's okay seeing three or four goals getting knocked in but not constantly, not every game. It's better going to away games where the teams have got to open up a wee bit. If they had said to you fifteen years ago Rangers are going to win all these games and nine in a row, you'd have snatched the hands off them. But see now that it's happening, it's not the same. Rangers are expected to hammer half a dozen goals in every other week at Ibrox and it doesn't help when people say Rangers won't lose a game this season. That's impossible. Even the greatest of people have off

days. Even I've been missing the odd game now and again, through work or whatever. In years past I would have made sure work wasn't getting in the way. I've seen the days when you would take sick leave, whatever, to get to a game but I don't do those things anymore. But now I find I'm saying I'm going to work to get some extra money, they're only playing whoever, and that can't be right.

Ronnie Bayne

I like to see Rangers compete in Europe but I wouldn't want them to leave Scottish football. But we should go back to the sixteen team league. I wouldn't want Rangers to pull out of Scottish football, we're a Scottish team. I suppose it's up to Hearts and Hibs and the like to come up to our level but I don't think that'll ever happen – in fact the gap's got bigger in the last 10–15 years.

Neil Cameron

No I'm not bored with the Premier League. I'm a traditionalist. I like my day out at the football. Our bus leaves a bit early and we have two or three beers, watch the game, two or three beers and then back home. There's not much you could do with the League, there's just not enough good teams in Scotland.

Ally Redford

I think Rangers and Celtic have subsidised Scottish football for years and I would like to see them leaving. But as for the football, to be honest, I don't think it's any worse than the English Premiership which is blown out of all proportion. People say there's only two teams in Scotland but that's no different to most leagues in Europe. The football Rangers have played since Advocaat came has been a joy to watch, although other teams make it difficult at times. Hearts at Ibrox were an absolute disgrace and must have been terrible for a neutral to watch.

Kirsty Paterson

I personally think that there are times when the SPL can get boring, especially when you've been through the excitement of a European tie one week and then have to go back to the joys of Dundee. I think a lot of Rangers fans would say that they are bored with it, but to be honest, at least you now what you have with the SPL – better the devil you know and all that.

Richard Pollock

This season I gave up my season ticket which I've had since about 1984, not entirely for money reasons. I'm just pissed off about the Premier League. It's been gradually getting worse over the years and it's just games involving Rangers. You watch other matches and they're reasonably open games but teams just come to Ibrox and defend and it's not much fun going to Ibrox any more. I'm not going to pay nearly £500 up front for a club deck seat to watch teams defend against Rangers, although saying that I do pay most weeks now to go into the Broomloan. I don't see much future for the Premier League. Rangers and Celtic are far too big for it. Even this Atlantic League they're talking about, I would take anything, anything. It's not the other clubs' fault – they haven't got the fans to generate the cash. But it's not our fault. So why should we be held back?

I would have no hesitation in pulling Rangers out of the Scottish game. I think we've carried a lot of them for far too long so I think it's maybe time we should be a bit more selfish.

I'm not very optimistic about Scottish football. I mean when they made it three points for a win you would have thought teams would have come out, because a draw is as good as a defeat with the two point difference but it's not made a change to teams coming to Ibrox at all. I don't know what you can do to change it. Some guys on our bus have become disillusioned with it all and also gave up their season tickets. The age group that goes makes a difference to attitudes now. People up to about twenty haven't seen Rangers lose that much so when they do lose, for instance, against Dundee, they get a bit hysterical.

Alan Urquhart

I would say the standard of football has improved a little but it is not that important to me. You're just going to follow your team. Your day out is important with your mates. It doesn't matter to me how much Rangers dominate, I still go for my day out, meeting your mates, a few drinks. It was a bigger deal years ago when Rangers won the League like the time at Aberdeen, but there's been no real challenge apart from Celtic. Teams like Hearts and Aberdeen – they used to be a big game at Ibrox. Now, apart from Celtic, it's just another game. I would change the Premier League to make it less games, to make Rangers play the other teams just twice. Four times a season is boring, even from the point of view of your day out. You would be going to different areas rather than just the same old places. I would do away with the League Cup – it doesn't bring any excitement any more. There is a difference now from maybe two or three years ago. You can go to places like St Johnstone, Dundee and Motherwell and you can get a ticket there. That didn't used to be the case. So maybe a lot of people have lost interest.

Dave Nicol

I think Rangers games are value for money but I don't know how other team's fans stump up for season tickets. The biggest problem is that most teams come to Ibrox to defend, packing their defence in order to stifle the game. But it rarely works.

Davie MacDonald

Entertainment value in the Premier League? Absolutely nil.

I sometimes take my boy to the games and he's bored after ten minutes. It's boring to watch but I'll still go every week.

Alan Morton

Scottish football – it's a joke. Scottish football is boring now. It's started to become a chore going to matches on a Saturday or a Wednesday. You know for a fact when you go there's going to be ten men strung along the back line and Rangers have to score in first ten or fifteen minutes to open the game up. I would get out of the SPL. Rangers have to leave and I think it will happen within two years. It's stagnating, it's tedious. You go to Ibrox and there's no atmosphere at all, it's dead. The only time people are on their feet is when Rangers score a goal.

David Collins

I'm not bored with winning all the time, oh no, I quite enjoy it. I love watching Rangers, I love it. I think the standard of the League is quite good. I watched them when Celtic won nine in a row. A lot of supporters didn't see this. I sit and listen to the people around me in the Copland Road stand, moaning and groaning, when they're getting beat or held to a draw. I say to them you want to have come when they were getting beat week in and week out. And a lot of them leave the ground before the end. I can't understand why they do that. I've never left early.

Allan McEwan

I think Rangers should get out of the Premier League. Our supporters club travel to Europe and the European action was what we were interested in this year and it was a big disappointment going out against Dortmund. And having to come back and play Kilmarnock on the Saturday, it was boring more than anything. Despite all the titles we've won in recent years – and we've been on top of Scottish football – four times a season against Dundee and Kilmarnock, it's definitely lost its value. When Souness first came and Rangers started winning trophies I mean winning the League Cup and the League, it was an unbelievable feeling. Going out of the League Cup this season to Aberdeen meant absolutely nothing, I have to say that. Now I think Rangers fans think if we win the League we're in the Champions League, it's just a means to an end. Rangers fans see the Italian League and the English Premier and they want to be involved in a League as competitive. I think the League has been restructured enough, they've tried everything. I think we've reached the end. I just don't know where it's going to go. I'm not optimistic about the future of Scottish football.

Harry McCallum

Premier League? I find myself at some games nearly falling asleep. At times you can hear a pin drop. When other teams come to Ibrox, it's ten men behind the ball and it's boring.

Stevie Mochrie

The SPL can try as many formats as they wish, they can have play offs, no relegation, splitting the league into two or whatever, but the bottom line for many Rangers fans, myself included, is that it will still produce little in entertainment value. Credibility has to be earned and the SPL is a long way from gaining any. Most teams come to Ibrox to try and frustrate Rangers and hit them on the break. Okay, we do get the odd upset, but that's the exception rather than the rule. I know fans who hate going to see Dunfermline or Motherwell and the like at Ibrox because they can read the script before they go. It's because it's Rangers and their love of the club that makes them go. The league is even different from ten years ago. Rangers are so far in front in every aspect of the game. The money they spend, the stadium, the support, the gap is growing year by year. It was harder to win the league ten years ago, now it's beat Celtic four times and that's it, game set and match.

RANGERS fans don't stand alone in their condemnation of Scottish football. Owners, managers, players and supporters of most teams have complained about the Scottish game, albeit for different reasons. Almost every club outside the Old Firm has a chance of being relegated nowadays and the calls for change have been driven mostly by the the financial implications of relegation. Thus, at the beginning of season 2000/01, in yet another attempt to reinvigorate the game in Scotland, there will be another two clubs added to the SPL to make it up to twelve. It is the latest in a long line of changes to the structure of the game which have included altering the size and format of the leagues and giving additional points for wins.[4]

However, changes to the Premier League structure may now be too little, too late for Rangers and Celtic as they look for a more permanent move into a European arena. SPL Chief Executive Roger Mitchell has admitted that, 'a European League of sorts is inevitable, certainly in the next three or four years.' Rangers Chairman David Murray concurred, saying, 'I've believed for some time now that there will be the Champions League then there will be other leagues below played on a zonal basis'.[5] It is not certain how a European league format would work in terms of clubs' domestic arrangements.

Another idea mooted has been the 'Atlantic League', a competition for clubs from the second tier of European football countries such as Holland, Portugal, Norway, Belgium and Scotland. Again, it is not certain how this league would affect existing European competitions or domestic league arrangements but the idea behind it is clear – to maximise television revenue in order to compete with clubs from the top European football countries of Italy, Spain, England, Germany and France.

It seems clear that most fans are fed-up with the standard of football and the lack of entertainment in the present SPL. So, what would the Ibrox supporters like to see in the future?

Richard Pollack

A few years ago when Coca Cola sponsored cups here and down south, I thought then there might be an opportunity to have a British Cup of sorts, but I don't think that's ever going to happen now. In fact I don't think the English teams need us. The only way that would happen would be though Sky television now. I think this Atlantic League has more of a chance than a European League with teams like Juventus, Milan, Man United and those types of teams. I don't see them giving up their domestic competitions. But with the Dutch and Belgian teams, they're in the same boat as the Scottish League, two or three teams winning everything. It's all hypothetical of course, but I think it could work especially if they keep the prices sensible.

Alan Urquhart

I think the Champions League format is about right at the moment. I wouldn't expand it any more. It would be too much for people like me who follow Rangers away in Europe. The European games were the highlight of my season, even better than the Celtic games. The European dimension has taken over for Rangers fans. It's become more focused on that.

Alan Morton

This Atlantic League, I'm not sure about that at all, I don't think it would take off. Apart for the Dutch teams the other teams like Rosenburg won't attract the fans. The big boys from Italy, Germany and England, that's the big stage, that's the type of League I would like to be in.

Gordon Graham

I'm with Mr Murray on this score. It's time we ditched the hangers on, the ones who are only there to take the money off us. I'd leave Scotland altogether. I'd love to see us in the English League but whether they would want us is another thing. I think Rangers as a team are a big enough draw. I hate to say it but whether they would look at the travelling fans full of drink is another matter. Of course they could always ban the away fans and show the games at Ibrox on the screens.

Allan McEwan

This Atlantic League they're talking about, I mean your average Rangers fan doesn't want to play against PSV or Rosenburg. They want to be playing AC Milan and the real top teams. I think the feeling is we'll play all this nonsense week in and week out but our aim is to be in Europe. But wherever the money is Rangers will go. Murray needs the money.

Harry McCallum

I would like to move to the English Premiership and leave Scotland altogether.

Brian Donaghy

I feel sorry for teams like Kilmarnock, who have spent money on their stadiums and things like that and now they're talking about Rangers and Celtic leaving to go to an Atlantic League. It's a load of nonsense. I'm surprised that Murray has came out and said he would support it. I'm strongly against it. There must be a hidden agenda. Let's be honest, it's second best. If you want to be a top team you have to play the top teams. I'd rather keep them in the present format of the Champions League, competing with the best, not Mickey Mouse stuff.

Dave Taylor

We have proved in the Champions League this season that we can live with and beat some of the best teams in Europe and the prospects of a British League or a European League is exciting and would only make us stronger and make it easier to attract better players. The only problem I see with Rangers and Celtic leaving Scotland is that the Scottish League would end up in a similar standing to the Finnish or Norwegian league.

Grant Aitchison

Atlantic League – I don't know. It would mean going to a lot less away games and I like going to the games. I go home and away. I go to European ties but you can't do that all the time. However, everybody wants to watch a better class of football so there's benefits both ways. If it was down to me, I would like to see Rangers in a British League. That would be an attractive option, watching Rangers playing the Man Uniteds and Liverpools every week.

Willie Buchan

I would like to see a British League. If we could go in with Leeds, Man United and Arsenal, maybe with ten teams like the SPL just now. But in truth, I don't think it will happen.

Charlie McIntyre

This North Atlantic League they're talking about is a non-starter. If we're not going to have our games every week then it's no good. At the end of the day that's what it's all about. It doesn't matter who Rangers are playing as far as I'm concerned I just want to get up on a Saturday morning, go through the rituals and get up the road to see Rangers. It's okay during the European Cup runs to go and see teams like Borussia Dortmund, the Bayerns and Parmas but at the end of the day, you're going to see Rangers. This Atlantic League will be Second Division Europe. I can foresee in ten years time I'll not be going to see Rangers, I'll be sitting watching them on television and that's not the same for me. If you're not there it's not the same.

Alan Park

I would like to see a bit more European involvement, maybe reshuffling the UEFA Cup to accommodate a European League. I think a lot of fans would look forward to going to these games. I wouldn't like to see them go out of Scotland altogether, although there are guys on my bus who wouldn't mind if Rangers binned Scotland.

Steve McLeod

I think it's important to keep a presence in Scotland, but the idea of a North Atlantic League could also have its attractions. The question would be how would this interact with the Champions League? They could perhaps run two, three or four zonal European Leagues and the winners of each one meet up at the end of the season in a semi final–final format. This keeps the concept of a European Cup, gives us a reasonable chance of winning it and guarantees a set number of glamour home ties throughout the season. In Scotland, we could perhaps run a second team and still compete in the usual competitions without knackering our top players in these matches. However, there are limitless opportunities for the future of football. I just worry that we will be steam-rollered into a poor arangement because those in power feel there is no viable alternative.

Ally Redford

I would like to see them in a European League, an extended Champions League rather than that Atlantic League which has been proposed. The teams in the Atlantic League, apart from a couple, are minnows against Rangers and Celtic.

Stevie Mochrie

The kind of dream league I want to see Rangers in is an expanded Champions League, say four divisions with sixteen teams in each division and if it was successful it could always be expanded. There are a lot of issues that may have to be addressed but I would love this sort of league. I don't see us at the moment in the top division but third is realistic and second is achievable. This, to me, is the future of football. Europe is where it's happening, not Fir Park or Dens Park.

Dave Nicol

A European Super League and possibly a World League is inevitable but I don't see Rangers leaving Scotland completely. I think the day may come when Rangers have one team to play domestically and another to play in the European League. But I suppose there's a danger that playing the Europeans thirty odd times a season might tarnish the romance of European football.

Colin Glass

I would like to see Rangers in a British or European League because they would improve, due to being tested more. All my English colleagues keep saying to me that they would love Rangers to join their league, but the media, the SFA and some of the Southamptons of this world would oppose it, I'm sure.

Richard Morier

I would be fighting tooth and nail to try and access the English Premier League where we would be guaranteed decent opposition almost every week. I am sure that after a years or so when they had adjusted to the style of English football Rangers would be challenging for honours.

Stuart Crichton

What fans must remember is that if we do move on, we won't have the instant success they might think and we won't dominate the way we do now. In fact, a move might take us back to the bad old days of the early 80s and I wonder how many fans would return to their closets then. All these factors have to be taken into account before decisions are made.

Garry Lynch

I'd keep Rangers in Scotland in some shape or form. I'm a bit selfish but in a British League, Rangers fans wouldn't get tickets for the away games and in a European league I couldn't justify taking three days off a fortnight to travel.

IT LOOKS like Rangers fans' present football diet of Premier League – Champions League – UEFA Cup, will end and there will be a major restructuring of Scottish, European and even World football.[6] But there is reason to doubt that the 'promised land' of European football will be a panacea for the ills of the SPL.

There is no guarantee that in any European league system, Rangers would be in the first division. There is the glib assumption when fans, or club officials, speak of European leagues, that it will entail playing AC Milan one week, Bayern Munich the next and Manchester United the week after that – but that simply won't be the case. If football leagues all over Europe were 'deserted' by their top teams, you would have to assume that Spanish, English, Italian, German, and French clubs, on ability and in terms of potential television viewers, would make up the top league. What would happen to the other clubs?

Would Rangers, as a club in a second or third tier league be able to sell their games to fans or television? If they struggle to sell out their Champions League games against the top sides such as Bayern Munich and PSV, which has happened in recent years, what chance will they have selling fans the prospect of Sparta Prague or Boavista? What if a top European league becomes a closed shop with no prospect of promotion, could interest be sustained in the long term?

The other alternative mooted, the Atlantic League system, is also full of flaws. The concept, initiated by PSV chief Harry van Raay is regarded by many as a poor man's Champions League. Rangers could find themselves in league sections with teams like Rosenborg and Brondby. Again, these games could find difficulty in attracting crowds to Ibrox. In addition, the top players would still be reluctant to come to Glasgow.

There is a danger that by turning European competitions

into league formats, which is what is slowly happening to the Champions League, then fans will soon tire of it. Indeed there is evidence to suggest that European football is not as well received in some countries as their domestic product. Fiorentina's Champions League match with Arsenal in September 1999 was 11,000 down on the Italian club's average league gates and and at the same stage of the competition Real Madrid could attract only 15,000 for their home game against Molde. And the only times casual spectators can get into Chelsea's Stamford Bridge is to watch the European ties.

What about the prospect of Rangers entering some sort of British League? Again that looks unlikely given the stubborness of the present English club chairmen to maintain the *status quo*. Of course if the top teams leave the English Premiership to join a European league, Rangers could be invited South but it would perhaps be another case of joining a second rate league. The whole issue of the future of football seems to inspire so many more questions than answers.

If the Old Firm leave Scottish football altogether or patronise it with 'second' teams how would that affect the domestic game? First it has to be recognised that the huge crowds that attend Ibrox and Parkhead mask the fact that Scottish football, in terms of spectators, is dying a slow death. At the beginning of the 1999/2000 season Clydebank attracted the grand total of twenty nine fans to their league game at Cappielow and their ability to survive must considered to be a modern day footballing miracle. Airdrie, with a brand new 10,000 capacity stadium, struggle to attract 2,000 to games. Aberdeen's average attendances have halved since the halcyon days of Alex Ferguson. The two Dundee teams, Kilmarnock and Motherwell all play to home gates which are equal to English second division sides like Wycombe Wanderers and Wigan. Only Hearts and Hibs, (apart from the Old Firm) regularly get home gates of over 10,000. It is arguable whether provincial teams will ever again be able to attract capacity crowds to their games. Even the visits of the Old Firm have lost their drawing power and huge gaps in the stands can be seen at most grounds when either Celtic or Rangers visit.

For all the business acumen supposedly floating about football, basic business practices seem to be ignored. The product is simply too expensive. Aberdeen, for one, have recognised this problem and have pledged to cut season ticket prices for season 2000/2001. St Johnstone reduced their prices to £5 for a rearranged game against Hibs and virtually doubled their crowd. It remains to be seen if clubs take these type of initiatives a step further in a serious bid to attract the fans back.

In the long term Scottish football will find its own level – perhaps slightly above the Irish League – where wages will reflect the money generated from attendances. Perhaps more importantly, there will be real competition for trophies which may encourage more people to return to the game

Of course within all these discussions of possible new competitions and their implications it should be noted that there has been no canvassing of the fans' opinions. They are expected to just turn up and pay regardless of what's on offer. Fans must realise they may have become dispensable. If television does take off in the way predicted, then clubs' shortfall in gate receipts may be compensated for by television money. Italian media mogul Silvio Berlusconi once said football clubs may have to open up their doors for nothing to get fans into stadiums to provide the atmosphere for television.[7] A statement which was once considered crazy may be nearer the truth than many may care to realise.

7

Rangers fans and the media

A SECTION of the Rangers fans are convinced that a media vendetta exists against the club and its supporters. Indeed, to some of the Ibrox faithful it is their most passionate topic of conversation.

But there is little evidence to suggest that Rangers or their fans got a particularly rough ride from the press for much of the last century. Bill Murray noted that, 'In the 1880s the *Scottish Athletic Journal* ran a systematic campaign against Rangers, but this was eventually patched up, and from then until the 1970s Rangers, with the brief exception of Cyril Horne in the 1950s, have certainly had little to complain about.'[1] It is perhaps not surprising given the make-up of the industry during that time period. The anti-Catholicism which permeated Scottish society also affected the newspaper industry.

Dominant Scottish newspapers like the *Scottish Daily Express*, the *Herald* and the *Sunday Post* were aligned to the Ibrox identity in that they were, 'all very much part of the Protestant Establishment, not least because all three were staunch Tory papers, with links to a strong Unionist identity'.[2] Certainly, the *Glasgow Herald* was sympathetic to the anti-

Catholic views which could be heard on the Ibrox terraces.[3] This kindred spirit unsurprisingly resulted in a reluctance to criticise the Establishment's football team or its fans.

But several important societal changes occurred which affected the implicit press support for the Ibrox club. The decline of the Scottish Tory vote, a changing newspaper market through the 60sand 70s, the editorialship of people like Arnold Kemp at the *Herald* and changing social attitudes all led to a challenge to the *status quo* in Scottish society.[4] Rangers were no longer considered a sacred cow.

After Rangers fans rioted at Newcastle in a Fairs Cities Cup tie in 1969, the Ibrox club and its supporters no longer enjoyed such unquestioning acceptance. Further trouble at places such as Barcelona (1972), however much provoked, and at Birmingham (1976) gave the Rangers fans a growing reputation for hooliganism. In addition, the religious identity of the Ibrox club came increasingly under fire, regarded as a negative link to the emerging horrors in Northern Ireland. Like the Protestant church leaders who turned on the Ibrox club, newspapers such as the *Evening Times*, the *Sunday Post* and the *Glasgow Herald* began the intermittent criticism of Rangers that prevailed throughout the 1970s.[5] There was little that the Rangers fans could complain about given that the hooliganism was blatant and the sectarianism of the club was worn by many supporters often as a badge of honour.

The more recent tension between Rangers fans and the media and especially the press, can be traced back to the Graeme Souness time at Ibrox. In Souness, the media, like the SFA and Scottish referees, found a headstrong adversary. There was almost constant friction between Souness and the media as the new player/manager felt increasingly threatened and undermined. Consequently, there were random bans for newspaper and television journalists and the relationship between club and the media never really improved until he left Ibrox.[6]

After Walter Smith took over Rangers' media tensions eased but although Johnston's signing had reduced the criticism of the Ibrox club's sectarianism, Rangers came in for a different type of carping. Poor performances on the European stage were criticised, as was the amount of money spent on the players who were producing them. Apart from season 92/93 when they were within one win of a Champions League final place, and although recent European performances under Dick Advocaat have improved Rangers credibility, the Ibrox European record has been abysmal.

Criticism of players and officials' behaviour surfaced from time to time such as the infamous, if slightly humorous, incident of Ian Durrant, Ted McMinn and Ally McCoist being arrested outside a kebab shop to the more recent furore that followed Rangers vice-chairman Donald Findlay being caught on video singing sectarian songs at a supporters club function after the 1999 Scottish Cup final win over Celtic. In addition, other incidents made the front pages of the newspapers such as the revelation of ex-Rangers keeper Andy Goram's Ulster links and the (ten year old) story of John Greig larking about with a Flute Band at a supporters' club in Canada.

The supporters have also come in for criticism for refusing to discard the last vestiges of Ibrox bigotry with their tasteless sectarian songs and chants. And fan trouble at places like Tottenham, Sunderland and Tranmere mirrored the depressingly similar antics of Newcastle and Birmingham.

In recent years the ideas of a media vendetta have found a welcome refuge in the Rangers fanzines. In the absence of the football issues which keep most fanzines thriving, such as lack of money, poor facilities, lack of success and boardroom squabbles, the perceived media bias has gained regular coverage. It would be difficult to find recent editions *Follow Follow* or *Number One* which didn't feature some criticism of the media and even the *Rangers Historian* has been caught up in the conspiracy theory.

Follow Follow has been waging an unrelenting battle against the media in Scotland almost from the first issue in 1988. Since then, perhaps not surprisingly, coinciding with the time of Souness at Ibrox, there has been the examination of and inquiry into every perceived media slight against Rangers and their fans. One fanzine contributor, urging retribution, asserted, 'I think its time that the support took on certain sections of the media. . . It strikes me that the club is not prepared to challenge these scum so it is up to us. 40,000 supporters is a lot of economic muscle, let's use it. If no action is taken then a boycott should be called.'[7]

In recent years the claims of anti-Rangers bias in the media have have become standard fare in the publication. In *Follow Follow* (98) several articles typify the sense of injustice felt by many fanzine contributors, 'There is clearly a campaign at the *Record/Mail* and there has been for some time now. . .', and, 'No wonder the media treat Rangers with utter contempt. They know that the Chairman's bottom line is pounds and pence and as long they throw a measure of sponsorship money into the Ibrox coffers, then they can go about their business with impunity. To see Rangers ball boys in sweatshirts sponsored by the *Daily Record* turns my stomach.'[8]

Number One takes the attacks on the media one stage further and a regular banner across the bottom of its pages urges fans to, 'Boycott the Daily Record and the Sunday Mail'.[9] There are similar calls for positive action from the club – '*Number One* would once again urge Chairman David Murray to sever all ties with the Mirror group and to ban all advertising of the Daily Rebel (*sic*) and the Sunday Liam (*sic*) within Ibrox including the ball boys' tracksuits. . . their next anti-Rangers stance is just around the corner – you know it and we know it.'[10]

Another contributor claimed, 'a media witch-hunt against all things Rangers continues, the latest victim being Lorenzo Amaruso' (for racist remarks to a Parma player in a European tie in 1999) and a 'disclaimer' added, 'the campaign to boycott the *Daily Record* and the *Sunday Mail* will continue. . . we will gladly extend the boycott to the 'Scum' (*Sun*) and the News of the Screws (*News of the World*)'.[11] The publication in recent years has has turned into something of a crusade against certain journalists in the Scottish media and the whole media issue has taken on a life of its own.

Even the usually more sober and staid *Rangers Historian* commented on the perceived persecution of Rangers. One editorial complained about, 'certain tabloids which base their sales pitch around anti-Rangers sensationalism. . . A full scale boycott of both the *Daily Record* and the Glasgow *Evening Times* by all friends of Rangers is the only answer'.

Given the contributors' cloak of anonymity, it would perhaps be expected that fanzines would go over the top on issues such as perceived media bias. But what are the feelings of other fans?

Angelique Shield

I think the media and the press in particular have a really negative view of Rangers fans. We're supposed to be bigoted Orangemen and Masons. They are mostly Celtic-minded. You only have to look at the way the press and media tried to blame Rangers for getting Hugh Dallas attacked (May 1999) and we were blamed for the trouble after that Old Firm game as well.

Jim Black

We seem to the whipping boys at present – for the Mirror Group in particular. These people seem to think we are bigoted louts who can't behave. It was stated that before the Parma game that Rangers fans took over the town square and the locals were frightened and intimidated and our lads brought shame to the Rangers name. But the people who print these reports in the papers are the same people who thought it was great when the Scotland fans took over the town and city squares in France at the 1998 World Cup. . . The Rangers name sells newspapers all over Britain and we will always have to be on our guard how to conduct ourselves for fear of condemnation from the media. I have been in company recently that has discussed a boycott of the papers that go out of their way to dig the dirt on Rangers and it might not be a bad idea if only for, say, a week to let them know the feelings of at least one section of the country.

Ronnie Bayne

Well, what you read in the paper, I'd say they think the majority of us are bigots, criticising us for the songs we sing and things like that. Some of it is justified but a lot of it is not. Like everything else there's one or two who let everyone down. That type of stuff sets us against the press. You pick the papers up and you read Gerry McNee who has never got anything good to say about Rangers and I suppose Celtic also, but that sells papers. I know a lot of people who won't buy the *News of the World* or the *Daily Record* because they think it's anti-Rangers. In saying that, the Rangers fans make it easy for the press with the songs they sing like 'Are you watching Fenian scum'. I mean that's crazy. I suppose if someone's listening to that on the television I don't think it comes across too clever. To be honest where we are in the Govan Stand not many sing it there. The majority of the fans are okay and sensible enough.

Allan Elder

I think that the majority of the Scottish press are a bunch of sensationalists who would do anything to get your 30p on your way to work in the morning. Their attitudes towards Rangers is that they are a vehicle to sell newspapers and nothing else. Some of the stunts they have tried to pull are laughable, like trying to link Charbonnier with the murderer . . . I think that the Rangers fans get a hard time from the Scottish press as we are constantly being vilified for singing 'sectarian' song and labelled as thugs.

Derek McLeod

The Scottish media hate Rangers. For example we beat PSV in Holland (1999) and because the press can't pick on the team they have to go about their support and the songs they were singing, how it wasn't right and how it was a disgrace. They have repeatedly commented on this when they can't slag off the team. . . And take the 2nd May Old Firm game (1999) when

Rangers won the League and Celtic fans went wild. Who gets the blame? Celtic and Rangers of course. They blamed Rangers for their singing and actions. I mean did we throw coins or run on to the pitch? And the Rangers huddle, they claimed it was terrible to mock Celtic's huddle. Have they got a copyright on it?. . . The media paint a picture of Rangers fans as thugs and Celtic fans as good guys, which is a totally unfair image. Did you know about the 35 Celtic fans who were arrested in Newcastle city centre at the Peter Beardsley testimonial? You probably didn't because the Celtic/Catholic dominated media don't report on such incidents involving their own kind. . . They'll fawn over the Tartan Army and talk about Celtic having 'The greatest fans in the World'. But as for us? Well, that's where we have to sing, 'no one likes us – we don't care'.

Kirsty Paterson

To be perfectly honest I think Rangers and their fans get a hard time from the Scottish media. It doesn't matter how well things go for Rangers or how well behaved the fans are – the papers will always find something bad to write about. I'd say Celtic have their critics as well, but again, I'd say Rangers tend to get the bad end of the coverage. For example in Old Firm games it's always Rangers fans who are the bigots according to the press although both clubs have their equal share.

Dave Nicol

I have a very low opinion of the Scottish media and the press especially. It seems to be open season on Rangers all year round. You would expect that any club which dominates their domestic league to become the target for the media and I think that is illustrated in England with Manchester United. But I still feel the level of criticism Rangers are subjected to is totally unwarranted. A few years ago the media would try and qualify their attacks on Rangers by stating that we did not sign Catholics. Then when we did start signing RCs, the criticism was changed to Scottish Catholics. Now there is no way Rangers can be criticised for their signing policies. With the club being squeaky clean, the media has turned its attention to the fans, denigrating them at every opportunity.

Celtic fans according to the media, sing folk songs which are a reflection of their Irish Catholic roots – Rangers fans however, only sing sectarian songs. . . Celtic, from the fans to the board, like to play the part of discriminated-against Irish victims. The media overcompensates because of this and thus are very wary of criticising Celtic.

Graham Donaldson

I think all Bears are generally classed as bigoted and bloated on success. . . there has been a general trend towards cheaper, less respectful shots at Rangers. Typical examples in recent years has been the vitriolic attacks on Donald Findlay and John Greig. Greig's photo was ten years old – if that's not mischief-making, what is? Even this season's Euro run was seen as a failure despite what we achieved – branded flops because we surrendered a two goal lead to previous champions?

Stephen McLeod

To be honest I find the words difficult to find that capture my despair with the way the media treat the club. As far as factual reporting of football goes it's fairly mundane. I rarely think we get a write up or a write down. The problem lies elsewhere – the way the media vilify the club's supporters is my first frustration. I've been to Europe, mixed with foreign fans, had a great social time and not a hint of trouble or arrest, and this is usually after a defeat, and come back to read that we were a disgrace. It's a little bizarre how each time we went to Parma the Italian players, management and media praised us lavishly yet the Scottish media couldn't share their enthusiasm one bit. The Donald Findlay/John Greig incidents for example were not anti-Catholic acts but were dressed up nothing short of Irish terrorism. The club needs to do more to protect Rangers against untruths and abuse that it gets in the media. Until certain individuals at the club decide to do this more aggressively I wonder about the long-term damage the media are doing to our club. At the minimum I would expect David Murray to avoid giving his bi-monthly exclusive interviews to papers that persistently badmouth the club.

Colin Glass

I have a very negative view of the media in Scotland because with one or two exceptions they hate Rangers. Hugh Keevins, Ian Archer, James Traynor, Graham Speirs, Gerry McNee rarely, if ever, give Rangers credit for the things we do well but slate the club for the things they do badly. . . and the fans are despised by the media every bit as much, if not more than, the club itself. They have romanticised the Celtic support and insulted us at every turn.

Dave Taylor

I have very strong feelings about the Scottish press and I haven't bought a *Daily Record, Sun, Sunday Mail* or *News of the World* for over a year. There are so many journalists who write for these papers with an obvious anti-Rangers agenda. The *Record* and the *Sun* will bring in lip reading experts to verify Amaruso's racist comments and demand that he be fined, banned and basically kicked out of Rangers. But when Scotland played England we had to put up with weeks of anti-English racism. We are all bigots and scum because we fly union flags and sing pro-British songs, but little gets said about a British club flying the Irish flag and singing about terrorist organisations which have killed many British soldiers.

Des Ward

The press in general are only human and as the Scottish public love an underdog then this is reflected as Rangers get slated at every opportunity. They slate Rangers for their players costing so much money but in European terms, the club hardly spends anything. . . the huge wages and transfer fees are the fault of the global market not Rangers.

Ian McHutchison

If Rangers play badly, win or lose, I not only expect to read about it I want to read about it. What I do not expect are prejudiced rantings. I can accept the criticism – Jesus, a lot of it is deserved, the press must be free to express themselves. However they also have a obligation to the truth.

Derek McAvoy

The media dislike Rangers fans and think all Bears are bigots. The coverage of Rangers winning the league at Parkhead (May 1999) summed up the media. Despite winning the league on the ground of our arch rivals, the press focused on how the Old Firm 'tarnished the name of Scottish football'. It was Celtic to blame, yet Rangers get the collective blame. Had it been the other way round Rangers would have got all the blame. I am concerned that the Mirror group now own First Press. Surely Rangers can set up their own company to set up and print their own publications. The association with the Mirror Group and especially the *Daily Record* and *Sunday Mail* is something that must stop.

SOME FANS display less animosity towards the media.

Stevie Mochrie

Rangers being the biggest club in Scotland are always going to get more headlines, so I suppose it's a backhanded compliment. The people who own most of the Scottish newspapers have no feelings one way or the other regarding Rangers making the headlines, as long as it sells the paper. I think there has been a change in press attitude. The Scottish press now spends more time writing about Rangers off-the-field activities than what's happening on it. Maybe it's because Rangers are constantly winning things. To write about us winning all the time must piss off a lot of the anti-Gers hacks.

Alan Urquhart

I think Rangers and their fans are treated not too bad by the media. I think they get a fair deal.

Peter McFarlane

I think you've got to remember that these papers are trying to get sales so anything about the Old Firm is bound to be helpful whether it's positive or negative or even whether it's true or not. I think there's a lot of wind-ups going on. I know there are many people who are against Rangers but I think you'll find they slag off Celtic as well. It's all part of the game. I mean, what are the radio and newspaper phone-ins for, if not to wind up the fans and stir some interest.

Andrew Kerr

I don't have any strong feelings on the media. I believe the Scottish media are equally fair, or unfair, to both halves of the Old Firm. Those who believe otherwise are paranoid.

Brian Whitelaw

The Scottish media in general loves to slag our clubs instead of promoting them. Their attitudes towards Rangers varies from bumlicking to backstabbing. I can never tell from one newspaper to the next whether they are pro-Rangers or anti-Rangers. There seems to be the same percentage of journalists who write nonsense about Celtic as there is who write nonsense about Rangers.

THE MEDIA obsession with football, at least in terms of the printed press, dates back over a hundred years. But the relationship between journalists and football people, once mutually beneficial, has changed.

Daily Record assistant editor (sports) Jim Traynor noted the differences from the time he was starting out on his journalistic career, 'The relationship between the journalists and managers twenty odd years ago was undoubtedly too cosy. I remember standing there when I was a rookie, sometimes you'd stand in the street waiting for a manager to come and talk to you, or standing in the corridor, you very rarely had a room to go to. When they deigned to come and speak to you, they were treated almost like Royalty by these reporters, one or two of whom are still about. They were cracking jokes with them and all that stuff and I always found that very uncomfortable and I never did that. Maybe I just came in at the time attitudes were changing. Sometimes I got myself into trouble with some of the older more recognised football writers. But I wasn't a straightforward football writer. I was doing general sport where you went and you questioned and you analysed. When you did the football on a Saturday or midweek, you wanted to question and say 'that doesn't make sense' and this was frowned upon. But I think that questioning attitudes now prevails, although too many football writers still tug the forelock. . . I can count on the fingers of one hand the number of football writers over the past thirty years I have any respect for, not that this will bother them any, but I don't think they did the job properly. Even young reporters coming through now they think it's great to get an audience with a top player or a top manager. They go and talk about it in the pub with their mates. I think too much respect is given to football players, managers, directors and chairman by football writers even though it's not to the same extent that it was before. . . You can't do that anyway, if you take how the games are analysed on the television, you can't then give a newspaper report that forgets all the bad points, whether it is down to managers' misjudgement or a player's inability, you can't ignore it.'[13]

Iain King, editor of First Press Publishing in Glasgow, confirmed the easy-going nature of the traditional club/journalist relationships – 'About twenty years ago it was basically lip service and journalists trotted up to Ibrox and Parkhead once a week and were fed the party line and walked away. But now with so much money being involved everything gets examined that bit more'.[14]

The high profile of football has resulted in stories like those mentioned earlier in the chapter concerning players and officials being elevated to the front pages of the newspapers. This has led to tensions between the news and sports sections. Traynor admitted, 'There's a big problem between sports departments and news rooms. About 90% of people who work on the sports desks don't like dealing with the news desks, say they don't have a particular phone number and don't help them and that's wrong because we're all in the same newspaper. It strains your relationship with the clubs, puts a terrible strain in your relationship. The Donald Findlay issue didn't because I thought Donald was wrong to do what he did that night. But I thought the John Greig one was different entirely. I can see decent people go to a supporters' function and be seduced by the atmosphere and have a few drinks and it's easier to take a small step into that, than it is to stand back and Celtic people have done the same. But I thought the John Greig thing bore no comparison to Donald Findlay's. You're talking here about a guy who's a QC and that was unacceptable behaviour which Donald Findlay admits. So I had no problems at all about going back to Ibrox because I think most decent people at Ibrox thought Donald Findlay had stepped over the mark. But you do have difficulty in going to clubs when the feature or whatever has done something which the players or manager or chairman or directors don't like, so you do have a lot of problems that way. Because we have to try and forge a relationship – and it's always a fraught relationship anyway and it can collapse with one critical word out of place – you hope you can talk your way through it and say that's why I wrote that because you did have a rotten game or your tactics were rubbish. But when the news do a story on a player, manager or chairman it's very hard to maintain the link. You have to understand it's a newspaper and if these people who have celebrity status do something ridiculous then we are entitled to write about it. But it does cause a lot of problems for sports guys.'[15]

King also notes the problems which football journalists can encounter – 'The problem is the news reporters. Because the Old Firm sell papers, you'll get them wading in and doing the likes of the John Greig story which makes the sports journalists' lives difficult. It makes it a hard job for them when they've got to go back to the stadium and do their work on the football after that type of exposé has been done on people's private lives. I think the fans probably don't understand the divide between sports and news or the flak you have to take when you go back. I was working with the *Sunday Mail* when the John Greig story came out and I was walking back into Ibrox waiting for some real trouble. I covered a game that day at Tynecastle where Rangers won 4-0 and I never knew a thing about it until that night when I saw it in the paper, which is generally the way it operates. People think you know about these things, but the news people suspect you would tip the guy off, so they keep things close to themselves. It was difficult when I went back to Ibrox'.[16]

Thus, in many ways it would be an easier life for football journalists if stories like Findlay and Greig didn't emerge. But

Rangers sometimes suffer from their high profile in Scottish society and from time to time news 'stories' do emerge and anger the Ibrox fans who look for ulterior motives. The front page article 'Keeper and the Killer' which attempted to link Rangers' French goalkeeper Lionel Charbonnier to a Glasgow gangster on the basis of a chance meeting and photograph at a race meeting, was little more than disgraceful opportunism, highlighting sensationalist gutter journalism at its worst.[17] However, many Rangers fans, amidst the confusion of who does what in newspapers, claim the sports journalists are all in on the anti-Rangers conspiracy. This perception has manifested itself in an aggressive attitude towards the press.

Traynor is one journalist who has been a target for a section of the Rangers support, and said, 'In Parma when Rangers played against them in 1998, the Scottish press were right beside the visiting supporters. And these Rangers fans were trying to get through the big cage and the abuse was unbelievable. I'm thick-skinned and I've heard it all before but the abuse that day was especially severe and vicious. There are times when I'm walking down a town where Rangers are playing abroad, I have to go back to the hotel because the abuse is too much. And even by saying that these people will take that as a victory. Another time was when Rangers played FC Hakka in a qualifying game in Finland. There were about 150-200 Rangers supporters in front of the press area. I had to move three times and the strange thing was the people who were trying to attack me, verbally and physically, were English, all wearing Rangers strips, Rangers tattoos and Red Hand of Ulster tattoos. It was the strangest thing'.[18]

Bill Leckie is another journalist who has felt the wrath of angry Rangers fans – 'I've had death threats from Rangers fans, fairly sensible sounding Rangers fans. One guy sent a fax after I had said Gascoigne shouldn't play for Rangers again after he had beaten up his wife. Five days later a fax came through on company notepaper, calling me a scum bag and telling me to check under my car and all that stuff. I phoned the company up and they took it very seriously and brought in a handwriting expert. They found the guy and came back to me and asked, what do you want to do with him? Do you want the guy sacked or whatever? It turns out he was 50 years old, three kids, had been working there for about twenty years, exemplary record, but was just bonkers when it came to Rangers. I said no I don't want his wife and kids to suffer. So they suspended him and he wrote a letter of apology. That scared me, I found that hard to take in.'[19]

The idea of fans attacking journalists for criticising their bad behaviour would be comical if it were not so serious. But most of the abuse is verbal and it is within the pages of the Rangers fanzines that the most vitriolic attacks on journalists take place. Traynor acknowledges the abuse he receives but is dismissive of the publications – 'There's a place for fanzines because there's nothing wrong with the fans having a go at the Establishment or the people who run their particular clubs. We should always question or challenge the Establishment whether it's the football club owner or the government or whatever, because if you don't challenge them then they'll just do what they want. But there's a couple of Rangers ones which are particularly offensive – they're not clever. The good fanzines are the one which are clever, they use a lot of irony and are actually quite astute, but the Rangers ones are just offensive, nothing intellectual at all, it's just really gutter stuff. It's vindictive attacks for no reason but that's fine, they're entitled to publish but I don't think those fanzines do anything to help the image of the Rangers fans at all. That's the problem, the minority are always the more vociferous than the majority because they've got to be heard. So when people do come to study the behaviour of fans they'll look at these things before they look at the vast majority of fans who are ordinary decent people'.[20]

Leckie also has a view on the fanzines – 'A lot of people in the fanzines criticise the team and the club, but that's meant to be okay because that's amongst themselves. Look at the spate of stories which the *Sunday Mail* mostly ran, about players and an ex-manager doing the flute business and all that. Now if I was the media man at Rangers and I was caught on camera doing the flute thing I'd be mortally embarrassed about the image that projected about the club. But instead the fans all turn in the way and say, "How dare they, that was amongst friends." So it's all right to do it among friends and your own type. It's this attitude of it's not what you do that's wrong, it's getting caught that's the problem.'[21]

Within the saturation coverage of the Old Firm, both sets of fans claim the media is biased against them. Celtic fans have long accused the press of being anti-Celtic and a typical view in the Celtic fanzine *Bhoyzone* claimed, 'There are only two or three publications where the club can be sure the editorial content is honest, well-intentioned and sympathetic – and none of these are national newspapers'.[22]

It is an ongoing debate between Old Firm fans as to which newspapers and journalists favour the other team with every word written or spoken being scrutinised for evidence of allegiance. Few journalists openly admit Old Firm devotion and there is certainly an unusual amount of 'supporters' of non-Old Firm teams within the media, which, if it were transported to the population at large, would result in a much fairer distribution of support amongst Scotland's clubs.

King is aware of the suspicion which abounds in Scottish football – 'One of the things which amused me was friends of mine abroad, they're proud to support their teams. I've a journalist friend who's an AC Milan fan and they're completely proud to say so. But you couldn't operate like that in the West of Scotland. If you did that there would be trouble, it's such a football daft city.'[23]

Leckie explained the problem of being a *bona fide* supporter of a team outwith the Old Firm – 'People try and guess from your opinion what religion you must be, which is a ridiculous situation to be in. In Scotland people are supposed to be on one side of the fence or the other. I do a lot of after dinner speaking and meet a lot of people and they say, "Come on, tell us, we're out for a beer, who do you really support?" I say, "St Mirren, genuinely," and then they say, "Which of the Old Firm do you prefer?" and then they try, "You're from Paisley then, so what school was it?" And then the final question they always hit you with when they've tried everything else is, "So which of the Old Firm do you hate slightly more!" '[24]

Rangers fans do have their critics in the media and there are journalists who are open in their dislike for a section of the Rangers support. Gerry McNee, a long time critic of Rangers and latterly of Celtic, described Rangers fans as 'knuckle draggers',[25] whilst Graham Speirs, noting their poor behaviour in Italy, described some of the supporters as a 'sub-species' – 'the absolute image of ignorance and prejudice'.[26] Stuart Cosgrove and Tam Cowan whether in their respective *Daily Record* columns or on their joint Saturday BBC radio show *Off the Ball* openly admit their animosity to all things Rangers.

Traynor is candid about his feelings on some of the Ibrox fans he encounters – 'I thought the behaviour at the Parma game, the first one (1998) was worse than the second time (1999). The behaviour of the Rangers fans in some of the places I've been has been appalling. They think that because they're not breaking shop windows or overturning cars, they're behaving well and that's not the case. If you walk down the town in which you live and there are visiting supporters in the main square or thoroughfare, drunk and falling about, stripped to the waist, shouting and screaming and verbally abusing women and young girls when they pass, is that acceptable behaviour? I don't think it is and that's what I've seen these people do and I've seen Celtic supporters do it as well.'[27]

Leckie's views on the Rangers support are equally negative and he displays a genuine bemusement when he notes, 'It's very odd that they've got this attitude, We Are the People, We Are the Biggest Thing in the World and God Save the Queen and they have such an inferiority complex and such a paranoia of what everybody thinks of them. That attitude 'No one likes us we don't care', that bugs me. They're the biggest, the richest the most successful, they've got everything going for them and yet claim everybody hates them. You're either with us or against us is the thing. I might write a match report saying how well they played, what a good manager Dick Advocaat is, how Arthur Numan's the best player I've ever seen in Scottish football and put a couple of lines at the bottom about why Rangers fans have to sing 'The Sash'. And they'll say, "You're a Fenian Bastard, you never say anything nice about Rangers. . ." What I do find is that people will phone up ranting and raving, absolutely going bonkers and I find the best thing to do is chat away. What it really comes down to is that they actually agree with some things you are saying but deny your right to say it. That's the biggest thing, you cannot criticise what their club does, because what their club does is right. . . What disturbs me most is when people start to write long complicated history lessons about what they are doing and why they are doing it. Celtic fans are exactly the same and I say, "You must be confusing me with somebody who gives a damn." What I say is I respect your right to believe in a Protestant country or a Catholic country or a republic or a monarchy or whatever you think. But keep it away from a place of entertainment. You don't go to the cinema and stand up and sing 'The Sash' or 'The Soldiers Song', so why do it at football? . . . It comes down to the sheep mentality. But I can quite understand people getting dragged along with it and I don't have too much of a problem with it. We all go to games and we get caught up in the atmosphere but it's the people who genuinely believe that when they go to watch Rangers or Celtic that they're there not to support a football team but to support a whole political cause. Why would people want to put so much effort into that?'[28]

If some Rangers fans think their club and themselves get a raw deal from the media, there can be no doubt that their rivals Celtic get similar treatment. The 1990s was a decade of disaster for the Parkhead team in many ways. The club received criticism on many diverse issues – boardroom troubles, takeover bids, fan boycotts, paedophile scandals, problems over the redevelopment of the ground, unhappy players and poor performances of the team – perfectly exemplified by the trauma of their shock Scottish Cup exit at the hands of Inverness Caledonian in February 2000. Celtic were lambasted from all sections of the Scottish and indeed British media.[29]

Journalists and broadcasters also criticise the bigotry some Celtic fans display. Bill Leckie described them as 'obnoxious and ungracious – all the while treating us to their full IRA megamix' and reproached the club for allowing this 'poison' to be construed as great backing for the team.[30] Indeed, Leckie is convinced that, 'Celtic fans are worse than ever in terms of the songs they sing and their attitudes. I find them quite disturbing sometimes.'[31] Traynor has also criticised Celtic fans – 'They revel in conspiracy theories' – and noted that too many of them are 'soft touches', continually duped by their heroes.[32] And in addition to having regular digs at Rangers, Cosgrove and Cowan give as much stick to Celtic and their fans. Indeed the turmoil at Parkhead in recent years has provided them with an abundance of material for their irreverant radio programme.[33]

Nevertheless, many Rangers fans don't accept the notion of impartiality and the issue for them remains whether the media consists of numerous closet Celtic fans.

Iain King dismisses that suggestion saying, 'The treatment given out by the press is pretty even-handed. The problem is when you grow up in the West of Scotland most of the people who are involved in the media, whether they profess to be St Mirren fans or Partick Thistle fans are secretly supporters of either side, but I think they are professional enough not to let that creep in when they are doing their job. . . Because of the way the newspaper market is, with such a competition for sales, they have to be more and more controversial. I think the actual football aspect of the media most fans will take and they will have their favourite broadcaster and journalists and they will have the guy that they don't like. When you're reporting games it's not the most important thing whether Rangers or Celtic score, it's whether you get your copy over on time or whether your lap top computer works. . . I got stick at Celtic Park and at Ibrox. I wrote a piece when Celtic won 4-0 at Hibs during Tommy Burns' first period at Parkhead and they were brilliant that day and I remember writing it was a display true to their heritage of attacking football and that sort of thing. I was going into Ibrox the next Friday and I got a lot of stick. I've had it walking through the car park at Parkhead, so you're probably doing all right if you get it from both sides.'[34]

From an English point of view there is no evidence of any anti-Rangers bias in Scotland. Journalist Simon Stone, an Englishman who has worked in Scotland says, 'The press are slightly pro-Rangers, definitely. The spin that people put on stories, if there is something bad happens to Celtic they get swamped by bad publicity whereas if it's Rangers, it isn't as prolonged and probably not as deep. . . The people who worked in the newspaper industry at all levels tended to come from the Protestant community which means there is still a lingering Protestant majority and that is one of the reasons that Rangers get dealt a slightly better hand by the media. . . so ideas of bias against Rangers is nonsense.'[35]

Media representation is important in terms of how a club and its fans are perceived and Rangers have suffered from some unfavourable exposure. Since the 1980s the standard Old Firm television documentary format has been to single out outspoken and sometimes drunk supporters, carefully select a few bigoted remarks and pass them off as typical Old Firm fans.[36] It is cheap and easy television and it merely confirms many people's beliefs about the vast majority of Celtic and Rangers supporters. On the other hand, media representation can be positive and the Tartan Army enjoy a much better reputation although certain similarities exist in both set of fans' attitudes and behaviour.[37]

But whilst perceptions and image can be shaped and manipulated[38] there is no doubt that at times, Rangers fans leave themselves wide open to valid criticism. The media point to the obvious hypocrisy involved when a team with many Catholic players in it, have their fans singing anti-Catholic songs. And the offensive lyrics to many of the Ibrox songs have also come under attack. But as many fans have explained in an earlier chapter, the issue of songs is very complex and we should be careful not to read too much into them. Football fans, imbibed with the mob mentality, are not nescessarily the most politically correct groups. Supporters find it difficult not to get caught up in the atmosphere at matches and it would be wrong to claim that 50,000 people singing 'The Sash' at Ibrox all believe in or even understand the lyrics. However, as we have seen, the gratuitous 'Fuck the Pope' and the 'Fenian Scum' references are a concern not only to the media but also to many fans. So much so that on occasions *Follow Follow* and *Number One* have published pleas to eradicate this type of language from the songs.[39]

There is virtually no crowd trouble with the 50,000 or so who attend matches at Ibrox but there remains a small hard core of away fans who have no respect for the club. This troublesome element in the Rangers travelling support has been highlighted and condemned by everyone at Ibrox and elsewhere since Newcastle in the late 1960s and consequently the club has become virtual outcasts from England. Middlesbrough's Robbie Mustoe became the latest English player to have his application for Rangers to play in his testimonial game refused on the grounds that the police don't want the Ibrox fans in the town.[40] Is this the fault of the media?

What about the more recent newspaper attacks on the club and their officials which inspired so much animosity from the Ibrox faithful? To an extent Rangers fans have a case. There can be no excuses for the 'Charbonnier – killer' type rubbish which is written to sell papers on the back of the Ibrox club's name. Unfortunately, newspaper circulation wars dictate that these 'stories' will crop up now and again. But there can also be no doubt that a leading QC, Tory party grandee and Rangers vice-chairman singing 'We're up to our knees in fenian blood' is news. The Old Firm sell papers and it is naive to think that if any Rangers player or official steps out of line that it will go unreported.

The Ibrox club has also been criticised by the media on other fronts such as poor European performances, lack of training facilities, ineffective signings and unhealthy obsession with money. Are these criticisms valid? Most Rangers fans would say yes and indeed it is in the fanzines where some of the most stinging criticism of the club on these issues is expressed.[41]

Thus the media issue displays, again, a complexity about

the attitude of the Ibrox support. As Leckie noted, despite the bluster of the 'no-one likes us we don't care' attitude, it is obvious many are concerned about the way they are perceived and about their image and the club's. What has shone through in talking to the supporters is that they feel they are often caught in the crossfire, being attacked by the media and their own club. And to an extent that is true. David Murray has voiced his criticism of the fans on several issues from the songs they sing to their lack of passion at Ibrox to their moans at ticket prices. Some fans feel the club should be less critical and more supportive of them. But there remains a section of the Rangers support who clearly thrive on the media animosity – which is one reason why the issue is set to run and run.

8

Memories are made of this . . .

FOR ALL the different views Rangers fans have on issues such as religion, politics and the media, what binds them together is the love of football and the love of the club. Rangers fans become Rangers fans for reasons numerous and various, but for many, one memory stands out which helped push them down the Ibrox path. Although the moment can be shared with thousands of other people, the induction into the Ibrox way is usually very personal. Most football fans love the chance to reminisce about great games and great players and they also look fondly back at what made them support their team. . .

Jim Morrison

My first ever live game was when I was nine and my dad took me to see Rangers playing the British Army at Ibrox. I remember it was one long walk from Pollokshaws down Haggs Road and all the way to Ibrox. On the way back I can still see my old dad hitchhiking a lift for us and he was successful. Some guy must have taken pity on this wee laddie out at that time of night and walking home freezing. I don't remember much about the game but I think Rangers won 2-0. All I knew was that I was with 'ma da' and

I was watching Glasgow Rangers. What a thrill for me that was and from that night I was hooked.

Tom Plunkett

I was taken to Ibrox for the first time by some Rangers supporters to a European game when I was only a wee lad – we lived south of Edinburgh and my dad did not follow football. I was lifted over and as I walked up stairway thirteen and reached the top I remember seeing the floodlights which were along the top of the stands then and viewing this awesome sight. I could feel the hairs on the back of my neck standing up as I was led down to our spot on the terracing which I subsequently stood at every time I went until the seating was put in. No words can describe this feeling when you first grace the mecca of football – I'm sure all true blues know exactly what I'm talking about.

Rab Smith

As a toddler I was taken to all the games by my father and grandfather on the Johnstone Rangers Supporters bus. In the mid fifties we'd go out of our way to Paisley to pick up a severely handicapped chap called John who could hardly walk and had no speech, yet he was standing there every week waiting to be picked up to see his beloved Rangers. I was crazy about Alex Scott and once I had a picture of him with me at the game. Ralph Brand and him came over to take a short corner and Alex winked at me. It was the closest I'd ever been to him and it gave me a great thrill. That moment is still very vivid in my memory.

Drew Failes

You could get a lift over the turnstiles when I first went to see Rangers but when we got too big, my mate Saucy Ross and me would go along the old railway tracks and put up sleepers and climb over the wall where the old smelly toilets used to be. Then, once we were in the Rangers end, we would go over to the railings beside the enclosure and go along the wall until we could jump into the stand. We would go round asking 'gonnae gie me yer boattle mister' and we'd take them down to the kiosk and and get three pence per bottle. We'd come back much richer than we went and would spend our money on single fags and American cream soda.

Stuart Daniels

Getting beat 7-1 by Celtic in the 1957 League Cup final sticks in my mind, collecting all the beer bottles. My father gave me a 'doing' not because I was at Hampden myself at only ten years old, but because Celtic beat the Rangers. I had a big carrot bag full of beer bottles, you could get money back on them in those days. I think even the police were throwing bottles that day, it was that rough. I'd never seen so much violence until Andy Cameron played the old Empire. I just remember the bottles landing around me, I was only ten, totally oblivious and naive to what was happening around me. I remember going to Ross County in a Scottish farmer's milk lorry in the early sixties and the game was off! Back down in the milk lorry and up at four o'clock the next morning to go back up. We won 2-0 when we eventually played.

Jim Black

One of my first memories was my first ever cup final away back in 1964 against Dundee. My father and my uncle took my cousin and myself that day and as usual we were at the very front of the terracing right at the trackside. I must have only been ten at the time and coming from a wee village in Ayrshire everything was exciting, the crowd, the singing, the new scarf, the mandatory rosette, the men with the carry-outs, the lot. Well, the game was not long started and I was paying more attention to what was going on around me. I noticed the ambulance men were busy with people getting wheeled away on stretchers and one man in particular caught my attention as he was hanging over this stretcher being sick and dying, as I thought. All of a sudden Rangers scored and the place erupted and what I will always remember is that chap getting up off the stretcher and dancing about behind the goals like a mad thing. The police got hold of him and bodily threw him back into the crowd. We won the cup that day, 3-1 and I can remember the team and the lap of honour but that man stands out the most.

Colin Glass

I grew up in a Dundee suburb with one sister who supported Dundee and another who supported United. Not wishing to display favouritism towards either sister, when I was in Primary One, I chose the team with the best colours – red, white and the most royal blue. My sister took me to see my first game six days before my eighth birthday, Saturday 12th December 1964. What amazed me was after being outnumbered throughout my short life, there was Rangers fans everywhere, most of them wearing scarves and rosettes. It was just brilliant. I can remember Jim Forrest scoring the first and Rangers winning 3-1. After that day, without a shadow of a doubt, I was hooked.

Eddie Wood

After what seemed like years of moaning and begging to go to Ibrox my old man relented. I could go as long as I did what I was told and caused no problems on the supporters bus. At ten years old you agree with anything as long as you get what you want. When Saturday arrived I was up at half past six, sitting at the kitchen table with my scarf on ready to go – although the bus didn't leave until two o'clock. My dad said I had to go with his mates – he couldn't take me because he was at the TA camp every weekend. Which was as good a name for the pub as any. My dad's mates, Ginger and Doods,

looked after me and for years I thought Doods had a terrible memory. From the first time I met him, I had to run to his mothers to get his flute, because he had forgotten it. Then he'd give me 2 shillings. Every week was the same. Little did I know that my dad had set me up. With five kids to feed and only one wage coming in, this was his way of giving me pocket money without causing any upset. I went everywhere in Scotland on the 'Brandy bus' and never paid to get in. All the boys on the bus had their 'lift'. It was great, walking down Helen Street knowing I had my 'lift' and watching all the other youngsters trying to get one of their own. What a feeling.

Stevie Mochrie

My first memory of Rangers is being taken to Kirkcaldy of all places to see Rangers play Raith Rovers. This was in the late sixties and I was more in awe of the crowd than the actual match. My dad had placed me on the wall below the main stand. My eternal memory is peering over the sky-blue disabled cars that were around at the time and the crowd cheering every time the ball hit one of them. I was wearing one of those old woollen scarves, the ones that irritate your skin rather than keep you warm. The noise to me was deafening when the teams came out of the tunnel and all those woolly scarves were being waved about. The score? I can't remember but I was a Gers fan from then on.

Alan Smith

I remember the daft things about going to Ibrox as a youngster in the late sixties. Nothing about the games themselves but I remember standing for what seemed like hours outside the pub waiting for my dad to come out before we boarded the supporters bus. And all the guys who had a good drink in them ruffling my hair and giving me a couple of bob. And I remember the colours of the strips. I always thought the keeper's yellow jersey was very distinct and the Rangers shirt was just so incredibly blue. Daft, isn't it?

Adam Elder

My dad took me to my first game in the late sixties against Aberdeen at Parkhead when I was seven or eight. And that was the start of what was to become a usual routine. I stood outside the pub waiting for about an hour for him to come out, then it was along to the bookies to do the same thing. But that first game was the Scottish Cup semi-final and Rangers won 6-1. I couldn't see a thing because I was too wee. At that time you were allowed carry-outs in the ground, so my dad took some cans out and put them on the ground. I had to balance on them to get a view. I can't remember anything much about the game but I think Jim Forrest got a hat-trick.

Alistair Walker

One of the most prominent early images was the 1972 Cup Winners Cup Final in Barcelona. I can remember listening to a transistor radio in bed to catch all the excitement. Moscow Dynamo came back with two late goals and the match was interrupted by several pitch invasions. But the Gers triumphed and coming eighteen months after the Ibrox disaster it perhaps helped end the period of mourning.

Stephen McLeod

My earliest memory of Rangers was a truly life-shaping experience! Living on a Scottish island in pre-Sky Sports, pre-replica kit days, football was a cheap and healthy passion which dominated the lives of myself, my family, and everyone else around us. My father was a Rangers fan and my mother a Celtic fan from Ireland. I supported whichever team got me a chocolate bar, let me stay up late or got me out of trouble; they were both as good as each other. The importance of choosing one team over the other became the first serious dilemma I ever had to face. But how do you make such a decision? There was only one way. Rangers were playing Celtic in a few days time and I decided whoever won would be my team. I had no idea who were the form team or what time it was to be played. There was no live coverage of the game but Archie McPherson would usually come on the telly at about 5 o'clock with a match report and show a goal from a game. I remember being glued to the telly to hear the result and it came through – Rangers 3 Celtic 0. The clip they showed was of Derek Parlane scoring Rangers' third goal. So that was that, I was six and I was a Rangers fan.

Gordon Masterton

My first Rangers game was in 1978 against Juventus when I was eight years old. It was before the stadium changed, so I well remember sitting in the Main Stand looking out at the large number of people on the terraces, the small pinpoints of light as they sparked their fags fascinated me. I do remember within minutes I was a Rangers supporter and that was it. The atmosphere, the passion, the whole experience was mind-blowing. I still use the scarf that my dad bought me at the game and I will continue to use it until Rangers Football Club win the European Champions League, when I fully intend to throw it on the pitch.

Angelique Shield

The first time I went to see the great Glasgow Rangers was in 1981, my four brothers took me to see the replay of the Scottish Cup final when we beat Dundee United 4-1. I was in awe of everything, players like Bobby Russell, John Macdonald and Davie Cooper, the atmosphere, the songs, and I spent most of the game on my big brothers' shoulders as I was too small to see. I knew then I would love this team for the rest of my life.

Ian McHutchison

The first time I can clearly remember seeing Rangers was about eleven years ago. It was a home match against St Mirren. We won 3-1 and it was a cold, icy and wet day in February. It took us five hours to drive to Glasgow as we had to stop every five or ten minutes to clear the ice from the windscreen. Before the match we had lunch in the Rolls Royce club just across from Ibrox and I was agog. I'd never seen so many Rangers fans, all of them singing. It was immense. The match itself was a blur, and before I knew it, I was on my way home. But in some ways those were the good old days. It really meant something to be a Rangers fan. We didn't go to every game demanding a win. We used to get joy from the victories.

Robert McElroy

I have been a fan for over forty years now but I have very hazy memories of my first contact with Rangers. I do remember a couple of things. I do remember being bored. I was no sooner sitting down and I would be asking my father when I would be going home. I do also remember going to the Rangers Sports days in the 50s when I was very young and once I got lost at Ibrox and my father coming in the main door to collect me. My father told me years later that this old fella whose knee I was sitting on at the main entrance was actually Bill Struth. . . I also recall being at a second eleven cup tie between Rangers and Forfar. Rangers won 7-0 and I was thinking that they were playing Celtic because I thought that Rangers played Celtic every week.

FANS REMEMBER their first Rangers experience and for many it is burnt deep into the soul. Gers fans also have that one special memory that has stuck with them and which typifies or sums up what being a Rangers fan is all about.

Jim Morrison

May 1969 and Rangers are away to Newcastle United. My brother works for Scottish Dairy Farmers in Helen Street in Govan. A bunch of guys in there run a bus to Newcastle and my brother gets me and my father-in-law tickets. Well, talk about a comedy show, this was unbelievable. We're hardly out of Glasgow and some guys are pissed to the gulls, puking on the bus – what a mess we had to travel in. Anyway, we arrive in Newcastle and the convenor lays down the law – 'this fucking bus is leaving at ten o'clock and if ye're no here, we're away withoot ye, right, hiv ye aw goat it?' And with that we leave for the stadium.

Utter chaos at the match. I watched the game from halfway up a floodlight and there was a guy right up the top pissing down on all of us. I'm sure if we had got hold of him that night we would have killed him.

Game over, we got humped 2-0, so its back to the bus. Guess what, everybody's back except the convenor's brother, so now there's panic in his voice. Everybody is screaming at him to go look for him. He does and what does the bus do, yes, that's right, we leave without him.

Jim Black

1972 and we have reached the final of the European Cup Winner's Cup. I am eighteen years old, serving my time as a baker. I'm skint and I'm in debt up to my eyes to my mother. My father is a skint as me and I am desperate to go to Barcelona. Some of my mates take out 'Provie' cheques to get there but I couldn't get my old dear to go to be my guarantor. My only hope is winning one of the competitions in the newspapers. The paper shop is only three doors away from the bakery where I work so on the Tuesday, when I finish work, along I go and buy a dozen *Daily Records* and take them home to fill in the entry forms. There I am flicking through the pages only to discover the competition is not in the paper until the Wednesday. Shit. Never mind, the chap in the shop has known me for years and back I trek with these dozen papers to explain my mistake and get a refund. Guess what, no refund, no sympathy – the guy is an Ayr United fan – and I'm left with only enough money to but two papers on the Wednesday. No luck in the competition, so no Barcelona. I, like many others, will always regret not being there that night but we can always hope we reach another European final and bring the big one back to Ibrox.

Colin Glass

This was probably my favourite game ever, because Celtic had a really good team then – far better than their present lot – and we beat them 3-2. But it was three going on seven. It was watched by 50,000 of them and 80,000 of us, there were 40,000 in the Rangers end alone that day. One of my mates went out at quarter past two to get a pie and couldn't force his way in until half time. It was a superb game of football between two

great sides. Everyone remembers Tam Forsyth scoring the winner but I remember Derek Parlane scoring an equaliser on his twentieth birthday and Alfie Conn giving McNeil yards of a start but still whipping the ball into the net only thirteen seconds into the second half.

Alistair Walker

Wherever you are in the world and you meet a Gers fan you immediately have a friend. I met a guy in a bar one night in Dublin, who had been telling his mates there he was a Thistle fan. When I said I was a bluenose the guy was so pleased to have met another Gers fan that we spent a couple of hours talking about all things blue. Being a Gers fan is a lifelong thing, it's the only constant the club have. Players come and go, coaches come and go but the supporters are there for life.

Derek McAvoy

The game I remember most was on my ninth birthday, 24th March 1984, League Cup Final at Hampden between Rangers and Celtic. Rangers won 3-2 courtesy of an Ally McCoist hat-trick. Inside the ground the Rangers end was magnificent, it was a sea of red, white and blue.

Pre-match, I remember Jock Wallace pulling out a green flag which the groundsman had placed at the wrong side of the halfway line. The match itself was excellent and the atmosphere was electric from start to finish. I didn't really know the words to the songs but by the end of the game I knew most of them. Rangers fans went through every emotion that day, cruising to victory but forced into extra time and it was a great relief when super Ally scored the winner. When big John McClelland went up to lift the Cup, I saw Rangers win a trophy first hand for the first time in my life. Until the day I die I will remember this game.

Iain Breslin

Souness's first real game in charge was a pre-season friendly at Tottenham. It was the sheer number of Bears that made that trip which was so amazing. We had a busload of about thirty from the small towns of Kinghorn and Burntisland in Fife. I have no idea about the actual official numbers at the game but I can tell you that I and a couple of thousand others never paid an entry fee. One of those big sliding doors with the rails on top gave way under the pressure of the crowd. I will always remember the scene as hundreds of Rangers fans walked under the door and into White Hart Lane as it was passed over their heads. I was sixteen years old at the time and the whole experience left me in no doubt about the potential that Rangers had.

Alan McNamara

We were playing Celtic at Ibrox, the game where Butcher, Woods and McAvennie were sent off. Anyway, we were down 2-0 at half time and around me there were guys actually crying, not to mention wishing they could get to the Celtic support, if you know what I mean. The teams come out at half time to a great reception and if Bears are true to their hearts, they will admit they we were hoping to keep the score down. That's not the way it turned out. Final score 2-2. Richard Gough scored his first goal which was also the equaliser. I joined those who had cried at half time, only this time it was with tears of joy. Graham Roberts had gone in goals for Woods, and after Goughy had scored we were all singing our lungs out and there was Graham conducting the Ibrox choir. The Celtic support just sat there, stunned. That day epitomised everything about Rangers, us the fans and in fact what football is all about. To have so many highs and lows in one game was amazing. Who the hell needs drugs when you can witness games like that, which don't just last a couple of hours, but a lifetime.

Tom Plunkett

I have thousands of great memories following the Gers but I do believe the best time I have ever had was the second game Mo Johnston played for us after turning down a return to Celtic. I had sent a letter of disapproval to Ibrox regarding his signing as I did not think he was suitable for our team. I believed it was just an attempt to erode our great Presbyterian history. However, after receiving a reply from Ibrox and realising that this was the way it was going to be in the future, I had to either reconcile with this fact or give up following my beloved team. I chose the latter and decided to return to Ibrox for his second game.

As always, I went along to the game with my best pal of thirty five years Tam 'Popsi' Porteous from Edinburgh. He was saying how he did not think

Johnston should be at Ibrox and he didn't care if he scored he would never ever cheer for him. Both were telling each other that it was not right that a man who had been sent off against us and had crossed himself as he was leaving the park, should be playing for us, and while we had to accept Rangers change in direction, we did not have to accept him as a player.

We watched the game and passed many comments regarding his tireless effort against his old team, but still held firm to the belief that he should be plying his trade elsewhere. The game's end to end. With a few minutes left on the clock, and both of us had resigned ourselves to 0-0. The ball was then centred to Mo. He kind of half hit the ball, but did enough to send it into the corner of the net, leaving the Celtic fans shell shocked.

Well, for two guys who swore they would never cheer for an ex-Tim, you should have seen this. We were doing cartwheels in the passageway and I felt a euphoria I had never felt before at an Old Firm game. Three quarters of Ibrox was bouncing up and down and, pointing to the Celtic support who were standing there gobsmacked and we were singing their old song, Mo, Mo, Super Mo, Super Maurice Johnston. This continued until the last Celtic fan had left the stadium. I have never seen or felt such a fantastic show from the Gers support which carried on out in the streets. I doubt I will ever get such a high again. No need to tell you our opinion of Mo was changed forever.

Brian Whitelaw

Funny enough, one of the most vivid memories of being a Rangers fan was one time when I was at a Celtic game! I had a Celtic supporting friend from Edinburgh and we got on well and we decided one night we would go to a game involving the other one's team. We went to the Rangers game first and it was uneventful. Then he decided that the game I had to go to was the Tims versus St Etienne in the European Cup. I think they were down 1-0 from the first leg in France. So we're standing behind the goal and just before half time, with the score 0-0, Celtic got a penalty. Tommy Gemmill spots the ball and as he runs back some big Neanderthal in front of me turns round and says, 'Say the first

two lines o' the rosary son, I've forgoat.' So I just look at him open mouthed, no words coming out and surrounded by thousands of the great unwashed. I was completely crapping myself. Jut then, big Tam steps up and blooters the ball into the net. The crowd went wild and so did I and the Neanderthal forgot all about me. It's probably the only time I have been delighted to see Celtic score.

Adam Elder

One of my favourite memories is my first away trip to see Rangers in Europe. It was the first full season with Souness in charge, 1986/87, and we played Borussia Moenchengladbach. We drew 1-1 at Ibrox and we went out after drawing 0-0 in Germany. My mate Johnny McKillop ran the bus and it was a brilliant journey over and back. I had been a bit short before going and my dad had helped me out with a few bob. But on the bus we got a card school going and my luck was in. I made a fortune and I ended up coming back with more money than I went with. I bought Blue Label vodka on the ferry for all the boys, and we were having a great time. On the way back I bought toys for my children – all this was off the card money. At the game, me and Johnny skipped into the stand and we were the only two Rangers fans in there and the Germans were asking us, 'who's that number seven' – it was Derek Ferguson. He was man of the match and Souness was brilliant as well. In fact the whole team played well, even though Stuart Munro and Davie Cooper got sent off and we ended up with nine men. But it wasn't to be.

Tanya Orr

Sitting in the Celtic end of the stand, due to getting the wrong tickets, in 1989 when Joe Miller scored the winner, stands out in my mind. It was an awful day. There was mum, dad and I, all sitting with our Rangers scarves in a plastic bag and trying to say very little as we were surrounded by thousands of Celtic fans. We tried very hard to keep quiet, well I did, my dad didn't, and not make ourselves look too obvious. This was going fine until Miller scored and were the only three in the Celtic end who were not on our feet singing and dancing. But thankfully we got out alive.

Stephen McLeod

I've received the greatest hospitality from Rangers supporters clubs all over Canada. I was at Parkhead in May 1999 when we won the League and I held the League Cup aloft in the District Bar in Kinning Park to the acclaim of Coisty, Durranty, Fergie and Stuart McCall. But my greatest moment was when I fulfilled my lifetime ambition and played for Rangers at Ibrox. Well, sort of. My mate Duncy and I left the Stadium bar at Ibrox one night and I decided to walk past the ground. It was at the time when they were building the new club deck and the ground was like a building site. Walking past we saw a wooden door flapping in the wind. It was a door leading into the corner of the Copland Road and East Enclosure. Well, that was that. In we went climbing down blocks of bricks, jumping, scurrying and then we were there, on the very corner of the pitch. I was worried about going on because these were the days of Alistair Hood and I didn't want my season ticket confiscated if I got caught. But it took about a nano second and it was a top of the voice charge to the centre circle. That was it, we were in the centre circle with the lights from the club deck illuminating the centre circle and not a nightwatchman in sight. So we set about having a little fun. First stop Duncy had to be Paddy Bonnar and go in goal at the Copland end for me to take a last minute penalty against Celtic to win the league. The invisible ball was flying into the corner. . . and it was there . . . the crowd were going wild . . . and I was running to the East Enclosure. . . and I was on my knees. Walter was running towards me with his arms in the air. After we'd been in the ground for about a half an hour we decided it was time to go. The souvenirs were gathered, a lump of turf and a yellow plastic goal peg, which I still have. On the way out we stopped off at the Copland Road stand so that Duncy could interview me for the TV public to find out how I had enjoyed my first dramatic yet successful season at Ibrox. . .

Garry Lynch

I've no problem in deciding what my favourite memory is – beating Aberdeen 2-0 at Ibrox to win the league. I was so pessimistic before that game. Aberdeen were a good team that season and we were on a poor run. Everybody was walking about outside Ibrox really charged up for the game. I couldn't stand still, I was terrified. I walked around Ibrox three times before the game started. I'm usually fairly optimistic but that day, I didn't think we were going to do it. We had half a team of the walking wounded. The spirit and determination of the team was brilliant and the Rangers support that day was just the best they've ever been. The fans at Ibrox are at their the best in adversity and I honestly believe they won the game for us. Usually, Rangers fans are the most fickle in the world and I argue with lots of punters at Ibrox for abusing the team. But that day every one of them deserved a medal.

Ian McHutchison

My favourite match was in the early 90s when we beat Celtic in a league Cup, or Coca Cola as I think it was then, semi-final at Ibrox. It finished 1-0 to us and Peter Huistra got sent off. It was amazing for me because it was my first time in the enclosure – what an experience. The banter never stopped all night and the worst abuse was reserved for Frank 'werzzaburds'

McAvennie, and even when he wasn't doing anything, he still got it and finally after having a right stinker he was taken off. Obviously we had got to him because as he walked off he flipped a digit straight at us and there was uproar. One guy took it personally, jumped the fence and went over to McAvennie and. . . ruffled his hair. It was a classic. The guy then legged it back into the enclosure amid shouts of 'hide him', . . . and we did.

Des Ward

The best memory I have of being a Rangers fan was watching the Rangers versus Marseilles match in the Champions League, when it was still for Champions, with my wee brother. He has always been an Aberdeen fan but we both jumped around the house when Sweggy scored that header and then when Hateley scored to equalise we went berserk. We should have made the final that year.

Gordon Masterton

The semi final against Celtic at Hampden in the mid nineties when Davie Robertson got sent off after a few minutes. I was in the North Enclosure that night and even with a man down Rangers were the far better team and long before we scored the supporters were singing that the game was easy.

Anyway, McCoist suddenly scored and the whole place went mental and I was jumping around on a couple of guys I didn't know. I turned round to see where my dad was and there he was seemingly holding back all the turmoil behind him, with a big grin on his face, both fists clenched and shaking in celebration. I think this is the way I'll remember my dad when he's gone, although hopefully not for some time yet.

Peter Ewart

Best experience ever? It's got to be a certain midweek night at Tannadice for the big nine. I wonder how many people have claimed to be at this game? I've got proof – my ticket signed by Ian Durrant who we met on the way to our seats. I'd managed to secure tickets about six weeks prior to the game, so at that stage it wasn't certain that the game would mean anything at all. After the balls up at home to Motherwell it was suddenly the most sought after match brief in years – on the way to the ground we were offered £500 for two tickets.

The game itself contained some pretty decent football. After eleven minutes a ball down the left channel, Charlie Miller crosses on the half volley and Laudrup powers in a bullet header. After that it was party all the way. There was no way we would lose it from there. We spent the remainder of the game standing on the seats, giving it laldy. The emotion at the final whistle was unprecedented, season ticket holders of thirty years behind us all reduced to tears, the best bouncy I can remember – it was the best feeling.

The George Fox stand emptied of the 'home' support, well about a third of it emptied, the remainder produced Gers tops, Union Jacks and stuff and joined the party. Of a crowd of 11,000 I'd say there were about 8,000 bears. Add to that the 3,500 that were locked out but were let onto the terracing to see the trophy lifted and there were more bears than there were seats. The ensuing night in Dundee simply topped it all off. First of all, Abertay University's students union. Picture about twenty of us conducting a mock huddle in the middle of the dance floor to 'Simply the best'

and 'Daydream believer'. There followed a fifty strong bouncy in the middle of Dundee at about four in the morning. Superb, well worth the hangover.

Kirsty Paterson

I remember the day we lost ten in a row up at Tannadice. I was having to sit in with the Dundee United supporters because there were no other tickets to be had. There was one United supporter in particular sitting behind my pal and I, screaming for the police whenever she suspected anyone of being a Rangers supporter in the wrong end. I lost count eventually of the number of fans she had thrown out of the ground. All I could do was sit tight and hope for the best, hoping that I wouldn't give myself away. About five minutes before the end, the Rangers supporters in the United end all started letting themselves be known, and it wasn't long before we were all singing away. The full time whistle went and there were supporters on the pitch, on top of the stands, everywhere, I've never seen anything quite like it. Out on the street, the place was packed as the squad got on to the team bus. Richard Gough got on to bus to the chorus of, 'When Gough goes up to lift the Scottish Cup, we'll be there.' I think every other player got a song sung as they got on as well. As the bus left, we went back to the car, stuck the scarves out of the window, and drove down from Dundee, prouder than ever to be Rangers supporters.

Dave Taylor

Winning the title back at Parkhead was especially sweet especially after we had suffered the 5-1 defeat earlier in the season. I couldn't get a ticket and had to make do with television. But I had to miss the last twenty minutes because I was getting married that year and had to attend classes at the Church – I took a lot of stick from my mates for that one. With Rangers 2-0 up and Celtic fans embarrassing themselves in front of a TV audience of millions I left secure in the knowledge that the League title was coming home. . . Then there was the cup final a few weeks later and after the game

had been won the sight of the whole Rangers end doing the bouncy is one that will live in my mind for ever.

Stuart Daniels

The game against Hearts last year when Rangers were celebrating being one hundred years at Ibrox. They brought on the old players at half-time and they showed you photos on the big screen of players who were no longer there. They showed you Davie Cooper's photo and I looked around and you could see the nostalgia in peoples eyes. I thought to myself what is nine in a row, it's nothing, if you could bring some of these greats back, the Davie Coopers the Davie Meiklejohns and the Jock Wallaces, just to see them walking down the tunnel. Seeing old Tiger Shaw coming out, wee Shearer coming out, that's what being a bluenose is all about, people around you, kith and kinship you know, the memories came flooding back.

Books

Adams, J. (ed) *Daily Record Book of Scottish Football no.3* (1972)

Bradley, J. *Ethnic and Religious Identity in Modern Scotland: Culture, Politics and Football* (1995)

Brown, A. McCrone, D. Paterson, L. & Surridge, P. *The Scottish Electorate:The 1997 General Election and beyond* (1999)

Brierly, P. & Macdonald, F. *Prospects for Scotland 2000* (1999)

Bruce, S. *No Pope of Rome; Militant Protestantism in modern Scotland* (1985)

Conn, D. *The Football Business* (1997)

Crampsey, R. *The First 100 Years* (1991)

Devine, T.M. (ed) *Scotland's Shame?* (2000)

Devine, T.M. *The Scottish Nation 1700-2000* (1999)

Devine, T.M. & Finlay, R.J. (eds) *Scotland in the 20th Century* (1996)

Dickson, T. & Treble, J.H. (eds) *People and Society in Scotland* (1992)

Dunleavy, P. Gamble, A. Holliday, I. Peele, G. *Developments in British Politics* (1993)

Ferrier, B. & McElroy, R. *Rangers: The Complete Record* (1996)

Forsyth, R. *Blue and True: Unforgettable Rangers Days* (1996)

Fynn, A. & Guest, L. *The Secret Life of Football* (1989)

Halliday, S. *Rangers: The Official Illustrated History* (1989)

Horton, E. *Moving the Goal Posts: Football's Exploitation* (1997)

Kelly, S. F. *Graeme Souness: A Soccer Revolutionary* (1994)

Kemp, A. (ed) *The Glasgow Herald Book of Scotland* (1990)

Jamieson, S. *Graeme Souness: The Ibrox revolution and the legacy of the Iron Lady's man* (1997)

Lugton, A. *The Making of Hibs* (1995)

McCrone, D. *Understanding Scotland: the sociology of a stateless nation* (1992)

Marshall, W. *The Billy Boys: A Concise History of Orangeism in Scotland* (1996)

Murray, W. *The Old Firm in the New Age: Celtic and Rangers since the Souness revolution* (1998)

Murray, W. *The Old Firm: Sectarianism, Sport and Society in Scotland* (1984)

Robinson, J (ed) *The Supporters Guide to Scottish Football 1998*

Spence, A. *Its Colours They Are Fine* (1977)

Walker, G. & Gallagher, T. (eds) *Sermons and Battle Hymns: Protestant Popular Culture in Modern Scotland* (1990)

Wilson, M. *Don't Cry For Me Argentina* (1998)

Sir Norman Chester Centre for football research *Seven Years on: Glasgow Rangers and Rangers Supporters 1983-1990*

Notes

Chapter 1 Introduction

1 Spence, A. *It's Colours They Are Fine* (1977)

2 Robinson, J. (ed) *The Supporters Guide to Scottish Football* 1998
shows that clubs like Motherwell, Hibs, Dundee, Aberdeen,
Falkirk, Dumbarton and Raith Rovers all had their biggest
crowds in the 1950s.

3 By the 1890s most of the major teams had groups of supporters
who paid a weekly subscription to hire a brake, usually a 24-
seater four-in-hand wagonette, which was hung with banners and
portraits of the favourite players of the time. As well as being the
most sociable way to get to a local match the brake clubs
functioned in similar ways to many modern day associations,
developing vigorous social aspects such as summer outings,
concerts, Christmas reunions and AGMs. However, the bulk of
brake club members were young, and in the early 20th century,
match days were not trouble free. The Rangers Jubilee brake
club employed an official bugler who was charged with creating a
nuisance at one match. There was a stigma attached to the
brake clubs. The term was almost always used in a pejorative
way, and gradually they disbanded.

Supporters clubs did not exist to any great extent again until
World War II. Several factors contributed to this situation.
Attendances were down due to unemployment and high
admission prices and in the twenties and thirties Rangers had
dominated the Scottish League, with severely adverse affects on
attendances including their own. The Rangers Supporters
Association can claim to be one of the earliest organisations of its
kind in Scotland. In 1946 officials from various individual
branches met in the City Halls in Bath Street (Glasgow) in a bid
to organise themselves into one body. In 1948 there were 98
branches with the majority coming from the Glasgow but there
were also branches in areas like Paisley, Greenock, Kilmarnock
and Motherwell, consisting of between twenty and sixty
members and 'based' in public houses.

The association was well organised, with individual branches
grouped into 'areas'. Area number two was in the southside of
Glasgow and in 1955 included eight branches from Cathcart,
Hutchesontown, Newton Mearns, Oatlands, Pollok,
Thornliebank, Pollokshaws and Shawlands. They also initiated
the Rangers 'rallies' which the association took up on and which
still continue to this day. (information quoted in R. Esplin, 'The

History of Scottish football supporters' associations', Dissertation Strathclyde University, 1999)

4 Rangers Association membership card (1948) showed the vast majority of the supporters clubs within the RSA came from the Glasgow area. More than forty years later an academic study 'Seven Years on : Glasgow Rangers and Rangers supporters 1983-9990' showed that only 37% of fans came from Glasgow (albeit Glasgow had by that time lost much of its previous population) 39% from the Strathclyde region and 24% from outside these areas. It is an indication that modern day Rangers fans are far more widespread.

5 Interview with Stuart Daniels 28/03/00

6 Interview with Garry Lynch 29/03/00

7 *Daily Record* 18/12/99

8 The exiles who moved to places like Canada, America and Australia during the 60s and 70s retained their allegiance to Ibrox from afar. Rangers supporters clubs were set up in these areas and for many it was a link with home. Ironically, better communications have meant that overseas fans can be in contact as much with the Ibrox club as fans living in Glasgow. In 1993 the North American Rangers Supporters Association (NARSA) was founded in Detroit Michigan at the instigation of Tom Plunkett, who had contacted Ibrox about the large numbers of supporters in North America. Nine member clubs were present at the first meeting in Detroit Michigan, some from as far away as Orange County, California and some as 'close' as London Ontario. NARSA now has well over 30 clubs in its association and regularly have Ibrox representatives at their annual conventions. The association also runs a company which is involved in the provision of matches via satellite with an annual turnover of hundreds of thousands of dollars. It is an organisation which has almost taken on a life of its own – a far cry from the days of the brake clubs. (Information from Tom Plunkett)

9 Technological advancement was important in galvanising NARSA and allowing it to function and prosper and it is technology which has facilitated the emergence of a 'virtual' Rangers supporters club, the 'Internetloyal'. It was Alan Rankin who formed the club, acting on an idea from several Rangers fans who were 'on-line' and it received recognition from Ibrox in June 1999. The club receives an allocation of tickets for matches and has members from South Africa, Germany and Denmark. (Information from Alan Rankin)

10 Rangers fans are clearly a disparate bunch and whilst researching this book I noted that fanzine editors, NARSA officials, RSA officials and other supporters club officials were not always aware of each other.

Chapter 2 Rangers Fans and Religion

1 Bruce, S. *No Pope of Rome:Militant Protestantism in Modern Scotland* (1985) p9

2 Marshall, W. *The Billy Boys: A Concise History of Orangeism in Scotland* (1996)

3 *ibid*

4 Crampsey, R. *The First 100 Years* (1991) p27

5 Lugton, A *The Making of Hibs* (1995) p24

6 Devine, T.M. *The Scottish Nation 1700-2000* (1999) p493

7 Murray, W. *The Old Firm in a New Age* (1998) p35

8 Murray, W. *The Old Firm: Sectarianism Sport and Society in Scotland* (1984) p12

9 Walker, G. 'Football and religious identity' in Walker, G. and Gallacher, T. (eds) *Sermons and Battle Hymns: Protestant popular culture in modern Scotland* (1990) pp 140-142

10 Quoted in Brown, C. 'Religion and secularisation' in Dickson, T. and Treble, J.H. (eds) *People and Society in Scotland* (1992) p71

11 Marshall, W. *The Billy Boys* p101

12 *ibid* p109

13 *ibid* p112

14 *ibid* p113

16 Devine, T.M. *The Scottish Nation 1700-2000* (1999) p383

17 Quoted in C Brown, 'Religion and secularisation' in Dickson, T. and Treble, J.H. (eds) *People and Society in Scotland* (1992) p71

18 Murray, W. *The Old Firm in a New Age* (1998) p238

19 *ibid* p239

20 Quoted in Brown, C. 'Religion and secularisation. . .' p765

21 Walker, G. *Varieties of Protestant Identity in Scotland in the Twentieth Century* edited by Devine, T.M. & Finlay, R.J. (1996) p264

22 Quoted in Brown,C. 'Religion and secularisation. . .' p66

23 Marshall, W. *The Billy Boys* p154

24 Quoted in Brown, C. 'Religion and secularisation . . .' p52

25 Brierly, P. & Macdonald, F. *Prospects for Scotland 2000* (1999) p16

26 *Scotland on Sunday* 5/12/99

27 Bradley, J. *Ethnic and religious identity in modern Scotland* (1995) p63

28 Devine, T.M. *The Scottish Nation 1700-2000* (1999) p504

29 Marshall, W. *The Billy Boys* p11

30 *ibid* p13

31 Devine, T.M. *The Scottish Nation 1700-2000* (1999) p505

32 Murray, W. *The Old Firm; Sectarianism Sport and Society in Scotland* (1984) p156

33 *ibid*

34 Marshall, W. *The Billy Boys* p203

35 *ibid* p272

36 Murray, W. *The Old Firm: Sectarianism Sport and Society in Scotland* (1984) p81
37 Marshall, W. *The Billy Boys* p154
38 *ibid* p55
39 Murray, W. *The Old Firm: Sectarianism Sport and Society in Scotland* (1984) p81
40 Murray, W. *The Old Firm in a New Age* (1998) p177
41 Jamieson, S. *Graeme Souness: The Ibrox revolution and the legacy of the Iron Lady's man* (1997) see Chapter 14
42 Murray, W. *The Old Firm: Sectarianism Sport and Society in Scotland* (1984) p222
43 *ibid* p223
44 *ibid* p234
45 *Daily Record* 3/9/99
46 Interview with Graham Walker 27/01/00
47 *Scotland on Sunday* 17/10/99 p12
48 Interview with Graham Walker 27/01/00
49 'Clash of the Titans' BBC2 27/9/99
50 Interview with Graham Walker 27/01/00

Chapter 3 Rangers Fans & Politics

1 Bradley, J. *Ethnic and religious identity in modern Scotland* (1995) Rangers fans polled indicated their preferences as Labour 33%, Conservative 32%, SNP 14%, Lib Dems 1%, Others 7%, None 14%
2 McCrone, D. *Understanding Scotland: The sociology of a stateless nation* (1992) p158
3 Walker, G. 'Varieties of Protestant Scottish identity' in Devine, T.M. and Finlay, R.J. *Scotland in the Twentieth Century* (1996) p260
4 Gamble, A, 'Territorial politics'in Dunleavy, P. Gamble, A. Holliday, I. Peele, G. (eds) Developments in British Politics (1993) p76
5 Ferrier, R. McElroy, R. *Rangers: The Complete Record* (1996) p6
6 Jamieson, S. *Graeme Souness: The Ibrox revolution and the legacy of the Iron Lady's man* (1997) p22
7 *Rangers Historian* volume 6 no. 9
8 Interview with Robert McElroy 16/11/99
9 Correspondence with editor of *Number One* fanzine 30/8/99
10 *Number One* no.89
11 *Follow Follow* no.104
12 *Follow Follow* no.99
13 It is debatable whether his resignation from Ibrox in May 1999 will lessen those Ibrox ties in the minds of the public.
14 Murray,W. *The Old Firm: Sectarianism, Sport and Society in Modern Scotland* (1984) p162

15 *Daily Record* 9/10/99

16 Cosmo Blue, Kelvinbridge in *Follow Follow* issue 29

17 see *Follow Follow* no.30

18 Walker, G. 'There's not a team like the Glasgow Rangers: Football and religious identity', in Walker, G. and Gallacher, T. (eds) *Sermons and Battle Hymns: Protestant popular culture in modern Scotland* (1990) p152

19 Marshall, W. *The Billy Boys: a concise history of Orangeism in Scotland* (1996) p139

20 Bradley, J. *Ethnic and religious identity in modern Scotland* (1995)

21 Walker, G. 'There's not a team like the Glasgow Rangers: Football and religious identity. . .' p152

22 Quoted in Anne Simpson's, 'The Thistle and the Shamrock' in A. Kemp (ed) *The Glasgow Herald Book of Scotland* 1990 p31

23 *Glaswegian* 26/8/99

24 Quoted in G. Walker's chapter 'Sectarian Tensions in Scotland: Social and Cultural dynamics and the politics of perception' in T.M.Devine (ed) *Scotland's Shame?* (1999)

25 *Number One* no.88

26 *Number One* no.87

27 *Follow Follow* no.29

28 *Follow Follow* no 95

29 See 'The road to Holyrood', in *Scotland on Sunday*'s 'The Story of a Nation' October, 1999. In 1979 a devolution bill had been defeated against a backdrop of confusion and controversy, not only of which political figures and parties were in support but also of the referendum criteria. Although 51.6% voted 'Yes', it was not the 40% of the total electorate which Westminster required. In 1999, the next attempt to secure a form of devolution was much more straightforward.

30 *ibid*

31 Murray, W. *The Old Firm in a New Age: Celtic and Rangers since the Souness revolution* (1998) p171. Murray alludes to the changing political values in Britain. There still lingers the perception that the Conservatives are the party of the businessmen whilst Labour are the party of the working man. This allows 'Celtic minded' business men like Brian Dempsey, Dominic Keane and Willie Haughey to square the circle of being free market businessmen whilst still proclaiming the socialist values of the Labour party.

32 In terms of voting through notions of religion, again the more interesting research may involve Celtic fans. Given their almost total devotion to the Labour Party – Bradley showed an incredible 85% support from Celtic fans – one must assume they recognise the religious aspect of their involvement with the organisation. It could be argued that if it were truly socialist

values which motivate Celtic fans (which is a claim that
dominates the rhetoric concerning the club's origins and ethos)
then Tommy Sheridan's Scottish Socialist Party, would be a
more natural bedfellow than the right of centre Labour.

33 *Scotland on Sunday* 20/2/2000

34 Bradley, J. *Ethnic and religious identity in modern Scotland* (1995)

Chapter 4 Rangers Fans & Scotland

1 This phenomenon is not peculiar to Rangers. In England there is
a well documented and deep rooted resentment of Manchester
United's success amongst the fans of the other 91 league teams.
In season 19998/99 this manifested itself with Manchester
United players being booed whilst playing for England. The
chant of 'Stand up if you hate Man U' was heard at several
games. Perhaps a better illustration of how the emerging culture
of disdain against United was the same chant being heard at an
England cricket ground during a test match. Consequently, in a
bizarre display of retribution United fans began to sing anti-
English songs at their games which initiated Man United/
England debates, slanging matches and arguments. This was a
subject of press articles, tv documentaries and radio 'phone ins'.
The country was divided when United took on England's
traditional enemies, the Germans, in the shape of Bayern
Munich, in the 1999 Champions League Cup final. Unlike
previous English finalists, Liverpool, Nottingham Forrest and
Aston Villa, who had enjoyed the backing of the majority of the
English, there was a large percentage who wanted the Germans
to win.

2 See *Daily Record* and *Sun* 27/03/98

3 See Ian Ferguson's *Fergie* (with Ken Gallacher) (1999)

4 See Graham Walker's *Sermons and Battle Hymns: Protestant
popular culture in modern Scotland* (1990)

5 Jamieson, S. 'The House on the Hill' chapter catalogues
Souness's problems with the football authorities in Scotland in
*Graeme Souness: The Ibrox revolution and the legacy of the
Iron Lady's man* (1997)

6 Quoted in Jamieson, S. (1997)

7 *Rangers Historian* Volume 2 no.5

8 *Rangers Historian* Volume 6 no.8

9 *Sunday Mail* 5/3/2000

10 *Daily Record* 2/3/2000. In season 1999/2000 there were around
forty overseas players who missed or were expected to miss
games due to international commitments

11 Rangers matchday programme 11/9/99

12 *Rangers News* 15/9/99

13 Wilson, M. *Don't Cry for me Argentina* (1998) p75. Although
the 1978 World Cup was a disaster for Scotland as a nation,

most of the top players emerged with their reputations intact.

14 *Daily Record* 6/10/99

15 The SFA have recognised this problem. In an attempt to generate a respectable crowd, ticket prices were reduced for Scotland's March 2000 friendly match against World Champions France in the official inauguration of the rebuilt Hampden Park.

Chapter 5 Money in the Game

1 Crampsey, R. *The First 100 Years* (1991) p159. There were other sources of income for Rangers. They initiated their own Pools operation in April 1964 and throughout Scotland, workers in factories and workshops, and not all Rangers fans, would contribute to the Ibrox coffers. The success of this operation was vital in terms of its contribution to the rebuilding of Ibrox.

2 Interview with Ian McColl 1/9/99

3 Forsyth, R. *Blue and True: Unforgettable Rangers Days* (1996) p143

4 Wilson, M. *Don't Cry for me Argentina* (1998) p104

5 Forsyth, R. *Blue and True: Unforgettable Rangers Days* (1996) p143

6 Crampsey, R. *The First 100 Years* (1992) p189

7 *ibid* p192

8 *ibid* p198

9 Adams, J. (ed) *Daily Record Book of Scottish Football* (1972) p9

10 Crampsey, R. *The First 100 Years* (1992) p218

11 *ibid* p222. Scottish clubs had participated in cup competitions in the early seventies backed by oil company Texaco and Dryborough breweries but those competitions were short-lived.

12 Williams, J. Sir Norman Chester Centre for football research *Seven Years on: Glasgow Rangers and Rangers supporters 1983-1990* (1991) p37

13 *ibid* p3

14 Fynn, A. and Guest, L. *The Secret Life of Football* (1989) p49

15 Halliday, S. *Rangers: The Official Illustrated History* (1989) p20

16 Jamieson, S. pp 29-30

17 Fynn, A. and Guest, L. *The Secret Life of Football* (1989) p49

18 Williams, J. Sir Norman Chester Centre for football research *Seven Years on: Glasgow Rangers and Rangers supporters 1983-1990* (1991) p3

19 Fynn, A. and Guest, L. *The Secret Life of Football* (1989) This sentiment underpins Fynn's whole argument.

20 Williams, J. Sir Norman Chester Centre for football research *Seven Years on: Glasgow Rangers and Rangers supporters 1983-9990* (1991) p23

21 *ibid* p20

22 Murray, W. *The Old Firm in the New Age: Celtic and Rangers since the Souness revolution* (1998) p60

23 *ibid* p111 – Newcastle United fans have recently found that such 'guarantees' are worthless. The Newcastle directors moved a section of the fans to accommodate corporate sponsors and were backed by the courts in their actions.

24 *ibid*

25 Rangers monthly magazine, June 1999

26 *Daily Record* 7/8/99

27 Rangers catalogue season 1999/2000

28 For many Rangers fans, Colin Hendry's signing typified the club's short-sighted policy of paying over the odds for a player with no resale value.

29 Interview with Tony Higgins 5/10/99

30 *Daily Record* 6/9/99

31 *The Herald* 7/9/99

32 Interview with Tony Higgins 5/10/99

Chapter 6   The Scottish Premier League and the future

1 Perhaps only Manchester United fans can identify with Rangers fans in these attitudes, given the English club's succss in Europe as well as in domestic competition.

2 Interview with Davie McDonald 2/11/99

3 Crampsey, R. (1991) p194

4 *ibid*

5 *Daily Record* 17/01/2000

6 Interview with Tony Higgins in which he raised the idea, now coming to the public's attention, of a World League. To facilitate such a competition FIFA have sounded out the possibilities of introducing a world football calendar running from February to November.

7 Quoted in *Four Four Two* September 1999

Chapter 7 Rangers fans and the media

1 Murray, W. *The Old Firm: Sectarianism Sport and Society in Scotland* 1984 p105-6

2 Correspondence from Raymond Boyle 22/2/00

3 *The Herald* would carry articles and leaders about the threat to Scottish identity posed by the Catholic Irish immigrants. (Jamieson, 1997, p139)

4 Raymond Boyle correspondence 22/2/00

5 Murray, W. *The Old Firm: Sectarianism Sport and Society in Scotland* (1984) p234

6 Murray, W. *The Old Firm in a New Age* (1998) p75

7 Contributor 'Hank Marvin' *Follow Follow* issue 39 April 1994

8 From contributors writing under the names 'CAS' and 'Forza Prod' *Follow Follow* issue 98 August 1999. See also editions 99, 100, and 101 for similar views. It is difficult to take the fanzines'

sensitivity to criticism too seriously when their publications are littered with references to 'Fenians', 'Tims', and 'Tarriers'.

9 *Number One* issue 90

10 *Number One* issue 88

11 *Number One* issue 94. Contributor was 'Rev Swine'.

12 *Rangers Historian* Volume 6 no.8

13 Interview with Jim Traynor 25/2/00

14 Interview with Iain King 18/2/00

15 Interview with Jim Traynor 25/2/00

16 Interview with Iain King 18/2/00

17 *Sunday Mail* 25/7/99

18 Interview with Jim Traynor 25/2/00

19 Interview with Bill Leckie 25/2/00

20 Interview with Jim Traynor 25/2/00

21 Interview with Bill Leckie 25/2/00

22 Celtic fanzine *Bhoyzone* Issue 22, August 1999

23 Interview with Iain King 18/2/00

24 Interview with Bill Leckie 25/2/00

25 Gerry McNee in *News of the World* 12/12/99

26 Graham Speirs *Scotland on Sunday* 29/8/99

27 Interview with Jim Traynor 25/2/00

28 Interview with Bill Leckie 25/2/00

29 The *Daily Record* (9/02/00) dedicated its front page to the game and didn't hold back from criticising the players or officials of the club. The twelve Celtic players 'few have performed as pathetically as that dozen' were named and shamed. The *Sun* (9/02/00) also led with the story and dedicated nine pages to the defeat and banner headlines were 'Get Lost Barnes'. It was a footballing disaster and the papers treated it a such. The following few days turned into something of a media feeding frenzy as once again Celtic sacked their manager, this time after only seven months and crashed into their perennial crisis. The English-based radio station *Talk Sport* had a two hour programme the following day dedicated to the 'Celtic crisis'. Sky Sports treated the news as a national tragedy and every sports news bulletin led with the story of the defeat.

30 Bill Leckie after Celtic's first game under new caretaker manager Kenny Dalglish against Dundee, Sunday 14/02/2000

31 Interview with Bill Leckie 25/2/00

32 Jim Traynor *Daily Record* 14/2/00

33 Cowan's column *Daily Record* 28/02/00 typifies his attitude to Celtic.

34 Interview with Iain King 18/2/00

35 Interview with Simon Stone 14/02/00

36 For examples see *Current Account* BBC Scotland, 20th May 1980, *Credo* LWT November 1980, *Football, Faith and Flutes* Channel 4 12 November 1995.

37 The Tartan Army, a hard core Scotland support who follow the national team all over the World, have had a good press over the years but there are many who are now less comfortable with their behaviour especially the rampant anti-English mentality. Traynor is no less critical of some of the Scotland supporters saying, 'Scottish fans tried to attack me at Rugby Park in a friendly match because I had written something about their behaviour in Monaco when Scotland played Estonia. Their behaviour was foul. The Tartan Army wouldn't say I was favourable towards them but they do get a good press. I don't think Rangers fans do anything that the Scottish fans don't do or the worst element of the Celtic fans don't do when they are abroad, which is get drunk, fall about the main squares in the town and shout at people and sing songs. It's unacceptable to these people who live in that town'.

38 Rangers have failed miserably over the years to foster a positive image and the club's humble non-sectarian roots have all but been forgotten. An aloof silence has been the defining characteristic of the club throughout its history and Rangers are currently seen by many as a cold-hearted money-orientated corporate business who treat their fans merely as customers.

39 See *Follow Follow* 98 and *Number One* 90. Articles 'Is it time to kill off Bobby Sands' and 'Are you watching Fenian Scum'.

40 *Daily Record* 2/2/00

41 There are numerous examples but see *Follow Follow* 59 and 98. See *Number One* 87 and 94 and *Rangers Historian* Volume 6 no. 10 for similar criticisms on all the issues mentioned.